TRUE TALES OF THE TIDE

An Angler's Lifelong Quest

TRUE TALES OF THE TIDE

An Angler's Lifelong Quest

by

MIKE HALPERIN

DORRANCE PUBLISHING CO., INC.
PITTSBURGH, PENNSYLVANIA 15222

ISBN: 978-1-4349-0148-4
Library of Congress Control Number: 2008928596

Printed in the United States of America

First Printing

For more information or to order additional books, please contact:
Dorrance Publishing Co., Inc.
701 Smithfield Street
Third Floor
Pittsburgh, Pennsylvania 15222
U.S.A.
1-800-788-7654
www.dorrancebookstore.com

Dedication

IT HAS BEEN SAID, "Life is like a coin. You can spend it any way you want, but you can only spend it once!" I am very glad to have spent a good portion of my life fishing in saltwater and experiencing the wondrous sites that can only be seen on our bays and oceans.

My wonderful wife, Nancy, deserves my eternal gratitude for her unselfish support of all my fishing endeavors. Over the years she has packed delightful lunches, awakened at all hours, waited up late, run to the dock with a camera, worried through long tournaments, and been there for me in every way imaginable. She has even gone boating and fishing with me for some of the adventures you are about to read. Nancy, thank you for always being there for me.

This book would also not be possible without the guidance, motivation, and constant love and support I received from my parents. From a very early age they introduced me to the joy of spending time outdoors on the ocean. We spent many weekends sailing from Great Kills Harbor in Staten Island on our family's forty-one foot Herschoff sailing sloop. On the deck of this boat in a life jacket and tethered to the mast with a ten-foot length of safety line, I was first exposed to the thrill of trolling for bluefish in the Atlantic or bottom fishing when the wind didn't cooperate. Thank you, Joe and Trude, for keeping me on the right road for all of those years and convincing me of the importance of a quality education.

*Fishermen, no matter what supreme good fortune be-
falls them, cannot ever be absolutely satisfied.*

—Zane Grey

Contents

Preface

WHEN I FIRST BEGAN to write this book, I hoped to share some great fishing stories from my years of experience. As the book evolved, I realized I should also share the wealth of angling information that has been passed to me so freely. In the chapters that follow, I have included details such as fishing methods and locations coupled with helpful angling tips and some special tricks of the trade. In spite of the persistent belief that most fishermen stretch the truth, each of the amazing adventures in this book is absolutely true—hence the title, *True Tales of the Tide.*

The only way I know to tell fishing stories is just as they took place. To my friends, I ask your understanding if a detail from long ago is forgotten. For the most part, everything is pretty much as it occurred, barring a touch of my less-than-perfect memory. *True Tales of the Tide* recounts a wide variety of saltwater fishing adventures, including the capture of flounder, striped bass, cobia, spot, Spanish mackerel, marlin, tuna, and sharks. Chapters vary from viewing whales at close quarters while fishing to a story on shark fishing that details how things can go awry when the Coast Guard is called upon for towing assistance. In one chapter, a state record dusky shark is caught when I receive an invitation to fish while my own boat is disabled. In one of the final chapters, I am able to help ensure the safe dockside arrival of the largest fish ever caught on rod and reel in the state of Virginia, a 1099-pound 12 ounce tiger shark.

I find it gratifying to watch as first-time anglers are coached to success. In line with this, numerous special angling skills and techniques are offered that can improve the chance of landing trophy fish. Whether you are a novice or a veteran angler, you will learn to appreciate the shared camaraderie of the angler's common quest and the continual need for greater challenge.

Anyone who enjoys the outdoors, fishes, aspires to fish, or enjoys reading adventure stories should readily relate to this adventure chronicle. If you enjoy saltwater fishing from pier, surf, or boat, this book is especially meant for you. It is my hope that you will be entertained, inspired, and armed with new fishing skills after hearing about angling success with some of the ocean's largest creatures. So come along for the excitement found in *True Tales of the Tide* as a myriad of fishing challenges are brought to life.

Wishing you tight lines, fair skies, and following seas as you pursue *your* challenges and angling dreams.

—Captain Mike Halperin

1

Hooked On Jaws

SOMEHOW I HAD MADE a real connection with one of my students who also loved to fish. Craig Paige had a passion for fishing, particularly shark fishing, in the late seventies and early eighties when it was really first taking off as the poor man's big game saltwater challenge. I loved it because it was exciting, it involved a controlled risk, and I never knew if I would land what I hooked. The possibilities of the type and size of shark were also almost limitless adding something special to the excitement.

When Craig said he would take me shark fishing for the first time, I jumped at the chance. I still remember him pulling up right before dawn with his seventeen-foot Renken on a trailer loaded with large rods and fishing gear. Off we went to Rudee Inlet and the Owls Creek boat ramp in Virginia Beach to launch what, for me, was an adventure of a lifetime. Craig had picked his day carefully. The sea was calm and was likely to remain so through at least the middle of the day. As we left the inlet he headed southeast toward the "4A" buoy, and the 90-horsepower outboard moved the Renken along quickly and smoothly. It was a perfect beginning to what was to be a glorious day.

Twenty miles and about an hour later, the "4A" buoy came into view and Craig slowed to an idle. The buoy lies 20 ¼ miles southeast from Rudee Inlet on a compass course of 149 degrees. This navigational aid is strategically placed about nine miles offshore from the most southern strip of beach in Virginia, lying just above the line separating Virginia from North Carolina. The buoy serves its main function of marking the westward extent of safe seagoing travel to keep all manner of north and south bound ships from running aground on

Virginia's southern shoals. More importantly for us, the "4A" buoy also visibly marks the edge of deep water just before the bottom rises to as little as four or five fathoms, creating a perfect migration and feeding route for large oceanic sharks.

I complimented Craig on his accurate dead reckoning in finding the buoy by running just time and compass heading. Before leaving the inlet, Craig had shown me how he scavenged bait from the fish remains at the charter boat fish cleaning area. There was a large dumpster where fish cleaners threw carcasses, heads, and entrails after cleaning fish for high-paying charter customers. Craig would use a gaff to fish the heads and discarded pieces of fish meat out of the dumpster. Bluefish and tuna heads were the best as they were really oily and worked well to attract the sharks we were after. Of course it was best to get these scraps right after the fish were cleaned late each day, but morning was okay if they were not too rotten and they were iced down to hold until use.

MY NEXT JOB would not be pleasant. Craig gave me a knife, a plywood bait board, and tuna scraps from the dumpster which I was to cut up into very small chunks as I sat in the bottom of the boat. The diced scraps would serve as chum once we began fishing. Lesson learned: never, *ever* wear any kind of clothes shark fishing that you want to wear again or elsewhere! While I did this, Craig opened a large ninety-six-quart Igloo cooler and started using a hatchet to chop up a semi-frozen fifty-pound bag of mink food (fish scraps) that we would also use for chum to attract the sharks. When done, Craig took one of the quarter bricks from the mink food bag, ripped the protective paper off it, dropped it in a five-gallon bucket that was drilled full of holes, tied it off on a stern cleat, and dropped it in the water. This served to set up a chum slick.

Next, my education was to begin on the proper rigging of baits for shark fishing. Craig used long leaders of plastic-coated steel cable that he would attach to double hook leaders of hand-twisted number 19 piano wire. I would later learn from Craig how he had made all of these rigs from scratch. They took considerable time, effort, and attention to detail to rig properly so that a large shark would remain hooked and also not tear up the side of a boat during the final moments of capture.

Craig picked up one of his two-hook 14/0 hook rigs and carefully hooked the top hook through a skipjack tuna head. He then positioned the second hook so it was buried in the meat still attached to the tuna head when it was discarded at the cleaning station. A fourteen-foot nylon-coated leader was attached to the baited two-hook rig, clipped into the rod, and slowly lowered to the bottom sixty feet below. Descent was fairly quick as together the bait and leader probably weighed two or three pounds. The reel was then set in free spool with the clicker on to prevent line from going out until a strike. Craig had preset the star drag on the reel to the precise tension where he wanted it before the first shark arrived and had a clothespin attached to the rod near the reel with rubber bands wrapped around the end of the clothespin to provide additional tension. This he clipped to the line just in front of the reel. The clothespin would hold the line on the reel against wind or drift but would come off instantly at a strike. This whole procedure was repeated with a second rod and reel, hooks, leader, and bait.

Now all we had to do was relax and wait. Craig turned on a portable radio and tuned it to a country western station with a deep bass beat. He said he thought that the deep vibrations against the hull and through the water might help attract the sharks. I was in favor of anything that helped, and besides I liked country western music!

THE CHUM STREAMED OUT. Craig had me throw a few small pieces of the diced tuna into the water every few seconds while the boat rocked gently on an almost calm sea as the sun beat down on us. After an hour I was hot and starting to get bored. I asked Craig if he'd mind if I lowered a line over the side to fish for any normal fish that might have gathered on the bottom or under the boat. I could tell from his facial expression that he did not really want any extra gear in the water that could ruin our chances of hooking or landing a shark. About the time I was debating whether or not to proceed with my spinning reel, the clicker on the 9/0 rod and reel in the stern corner of the boat began to go off with a steady clicking sound, breaking the boredom and signaling a legitimate sharp-toothed customer!

Craig told me to pick up the rod, point it in the direction the fish was pulling, and reel down until the line came tight. Then he commanded me to strike the fish hard three times in succession, each time keeping my thumbs locked down on the line on the reel spool while lifting up with the rod. I had never felt anything like that strike. I was powerless to stop the fish as it steadily took line even against my locked thumbs and the strong drag resistance on the reel.

"That's okay," Craig coached. "Just let him run until he stops and then we'll try to regain some line."

This fish apparently had no intention of stopping or tiring any time soon. He just continued to steadily remove large quantities of 80-pound Dacron line from the Penn reel while I hung on for dear life.

Eventually the fish did stop some two hundred or so yards from the boat, and I was able to start to slowly pump the rod and gain line back inch by grudging inch. Unfortunately, every fifty yards or so the fish would take off on another tear, and I would have to start all over again each time he ran from the boat. By now Craig had instructed me to sit on his improvised fighting chair—a ninety-six-quart Igloo cooler he had moved to the center of his cockpit area—and I placed the gimbal notch of the rod on the hard plastic flange that stuck out from the end of the cooler near its top. Not a fighting chair in the true sense, but an arrangement that certainly provided me with increased leverage to work the rod against the fish and, I hoped, save some of my strength. With Craig's expert coaching and my continued patient retrieval of line, eventually the fish came to the surface and began to circle the still anchored boat. Even though I saw stripes on the fish, I waited for Craig to identify the shark.

"It's a tiger shark and a real nice one, at least several hundred pounds! Just keep doing what you are doing and don't give him slack. Either he is taking line or you are getting it back."

That sounded good to me as my arms were starting to stiffen and approach cramping. I used the leather shoulder harness I was in to periodically support the rod while I shook out my arms and rested them. I could tell that I would lose this fight without the help of the gimbal belt, shoulder harness, and makeshift "fighting chair" cooler.

As the tug-of-war resumed, I was forced to stand and lift the rod up high to clear the windshield each time the fish headed toward the bow of the boat. Craig furnished words of encouragement as he could see that I was beginning to tire.

"Keep the rod tip lower as the fish gets near the boat. Don't give him any slack." Giving this shark "slack" did not seem to be a realistic option as he kept pulling on the line like an angry bull. To my advantage, he was now on the surface and we did not have to guess what he was doing.

Craig's rod was a great help in the fight as he had modified it to have a short butt. This effectively increased the pulling leverage of the angler as the shorter length of the rod made it easier to exert more pressure on the hooked game fish.

After more than an hour had passed, the shark was within fifty feet of the boat.

"Mike, I think he's starting to get tired. Don't give him any slack or he may get a second wind and get away from us."

"Yeah, well what about my wind? It's about gone!" Knowing I was close to victory, I fought through cramped biceps and fatigued muscles to literally winch the fish within reach of the boat.

"Just a few more feet, Mike, and I think I can grab the leader. When I say *now*, I want you to slack off on the star drag and put the rod in the gunwale rod holder. Then you can help me control the fish."

Craig already had on a pair of thick leather gloves and was leaning out over the side of the boat to reach for the cable leader. As he grabbed the leader, he yelled loudly, "Now!"

I quickly loosened the star drag and slipped the rod into the forward port side gunwale rod holder. As I already was wearing my own pair of leather gloves, I joined Craig in holding on to the leader so we could get the now highly agitated shark to settle down.

After about five minutes of holding on, we were ready to capture the fish.

"Now, Mike, you're going to have to hold the fish on your own while I tail rope him."

"You can't be serious! This fish must weigh at least three times what I do. What if I can't hold him?"

"Just let him go. You'll pick up the rod again, tighten the drag, and reel him back in. That's why we left it in the rod holder in light drag."

As I held the leader, Craig grabbed the shark's long scythe-like upper tail lobe in his right hand while he used his left to work the loop of his nylon tail rope over the tail. He was careful to keep the tail submerged in its natural position in the water.

"Don't let him roll up in the leader. If he does it too many times, he'll reach the line and we could lose him. Also, note that I never want to lift his tail out of the water or he'll go berserk."

Once he got the loop over the entire tail, Craig turned to me.

"Okay, I'm about to jerk this rope tight on his tail. When I do it, I'm gonna try to take a quick wrap on the stern cleat and hold on. Either way, when I pull the rope tight, the fish will go crazy. I'll need you to drop the leader and help me hold on to the rope until he settles down."

Never having done anything this dangerous, I was naturally apprehensive. Since Craig said he had done this plenty of times, I assumed he knew what he was doing, as risky as it sounded.

Craig quickly leaned back and pulled on the rope. I jumped in next to him and grabbed the back end of the rope. As predicted, the shark went wild. It was thrashing furiously and began beating its tail against the side of the boat. Craig had been able to get one turn on the cleat and this had elevated the shark's tail out of the water, somewhat reducing his ability to create mayhem.

As we held on to the shark, waiting for him to calm down, Craig had a new pronouncement to make, "Now that you know what to do, next time, you get to tail rope your own shark. I did it for you today because it was your first time!"

What a cheery thought! As hard as it was to hold the leader, tail roping the shark on my own sounded even scarier.

As the shark quieted down, Craig asked me to help lift the fish's tail even higher out of the water, and then we looped the tail rope tightly around the stern cleat. A second tail rope was added to make sure that our tiger shark didn't work his way free.

Since Craig had let me have the first fish, he was now anxious to return to shark fishing. The two of us baited a new hook and leader rig and both of the rods were placed back in the water. I could not imagine a second large shark hanging around this area since we had just caught a very big specimen. Craig, however, had different ideas.

Within forty-five minutes we had another strong run off on the larger 130-pound outfit. Craig reared back hard on the rod and was hooked up with what appeared to be another huge fish. As I cleared the second rig out of the way, I observed his reeling and pumping technique, and he was in fact doing everything just the way he had coached me to do it.

In short order his hard work paid off and a second shark with dark stripes took the battle from the depths to the surface. Another tiger shark was hooked up. Craig sat on the Igloo cooler and used the plastic tie down piece for a gimbal notch as he fought his fish.

The drill I had just been through repeated itself as the shark repeatedly circled the boat. Once the fish tired sufficiently, Craig and I used the same capture techniques to secure his fish as we used on mine. By the time it was ten-thirty in the morning, there were two long shark tails sticking up from the port and starboard stern cleats of Craig's boat, each tied off securely with a double tail rope.

CRAIG STOOD in the middle of the boat staring at the two tiger sharks.

"I really don't want to bring both of these fish in. I can't tell which one is bigger. Mike, are you sure you want yours?"

I think Craig could tell from the look on my face that I really did not want to release my first ever shark citation. It was also the largest fish I had ever caught to date.

"I don't want to let this fish go. Maybe we could bring both in?"

"I know what we can do. Let me get on the radio and see if someone can help us bring in these two sharks. I'm just worried about running out of gas on the way in towing this much weight."

I was greatly encouraged knowing that we would probably find a way to bring both fish to the scales at the dock.

Craig turned on the VHF radio to channel 16 and listened for a moment. As there was no active radio traffic he pressed the transmit button on his microphone. "Any boat near the '4A' buoy area or southeast lumps, come back to the *Bluefin II*. I am anchored next to the '4A' buoy and request assistance in getting two very large fish to Rudee Inlet so I don't run out of gas. Over."

We waited for a reply, but none came.

For the next fifteen minutes, Craig and I discussed whether we should turn one of the fish loose so we would have a better chance of making it to Rudee Inlet without running out of gas. Craig did not want me to lose my citation, but he also did not want to give up the equally nice shark he had caught. We were in a real dilemma.

Suddenly, appearing unexpectedly out of the morning haze, a large white-hulled sportfisherman with a flying bridge came charging toward us at full speed. When he finally throttled down to idle speed, his large wake hit us and started to rock the boat from side to side. The captain crept closer and closer with his boat, staring at the two shark tails sticking up from the stern cleats where they were secured. After circling our boat and coming within hailing range he called out to us.

"Where are the two tuna you need help with?"

"We don't have any tuna, just two large tiger sharks. Can you help us tow one in to Rudee Inlet?"

This revelation caused a secretive muffled conference between the two anglers who were up on the flying bridge of the boat. Then came an unexpected reply.

"Sorry, can't help you."

And with that declaration, the captain gunned his boat back up on plane and took off just as fast as he had arrived. A real swell man of the sea, we both thought!

Craig and I looked at each other trying to process and comprehend what had just taken place.

"Mike, I think he must have heard us on the radio and confused my boat, *Bluefin II,* with two tuna. He probably only came over to see the two tuna he thought we had caught."

Another strategy discussion was held and a decision was made to go ahead and tow both fish back to be weighed in. Craig reasoned that if he did run out of gas it would occur only a mile or two from Rudee Inlet, and we would then be in the major return lanes for all of the private and charter boats returning to the inlet. He was certain that someone would stop and help us then if they saw us dead in the water with the two sharks.

As it turned out, about half way through a long slow tow, a second fishing boat did help us by towing one of the sharks the rest of the distance to port. We made it to the weigh station at Fisherman's Wharf Marina without running out of gas. I think the slow speed we were forced to go in conjunction with calm seas saved the day for us.

AT WEIGH IN Craig's tiger shark weighed 539 ½ pounds while mine tipped the scales at 517 pounds. My appetite for finding, hooking, and landing large sharks and other game fish had now been whetted forever, and I was the one who was hooked.

Captain's Tip: Always be sure to carry plenty of gasoline and try to leave a reserve of at least one third of a tank or carry extra if safe and feasible. Also, don't rely on other anglers to get you out of a situation you get yourself into.

Captain's Note: Craig Paige enhanced his enthusiasm for fishing by earning his commercial Coast Guard captain's license. He currently runs the charter boat *Paige II* from Lynnhaven Inlet in Virginia Beach. Craig has earned master angler status from the Virginia Saltwater Fishing Tournament and has become a specialist in catching trophy size flounder using live bait. He has recently been featured in a flounder fishing show on ESPN with George Poveromo from *Saltwater Sportsman* magazine.

The author and his first shark, a 517-pound tiger shark

2

A Double Back Double Citation Day

My WIFE WAS SITTING directly across from me at the kitchen table.

"I'm getting my hair done this Thursday, and I will be out for most of the morning." Nancy's morning pronouncement at breakfast was music to my ears. As soon as the phrase "out for most of the morning" had crossed her lips, the words "fishing trip" registered in my private mental calendar. Quickly I responded to my wife. "I'm sure I can think of something to do on my own that day."

I began to plan my day off enthusiastically. I call it a day off because even though I am now retired, a day off on your own is truly a day off! Having been retired a little over five years, Nancy and I have "happily" spent many days together doing house projects and working on our "honey-do" lists. Although we thoroughly enjoy each other's company, this would be yet another chance for a great fishing excursion!

Naturally I checked the weather in advance—it was to be a clear, calm, and unseasonably warm early November day. The high temperature was forecast for the low 80s. I could not have ordered a nicer day.

On the night before "hair day" and "fishing day," I packed my lunch, as thoughts of local fishing expert Bill Sugg's mantra "FISH PEAKS, FISH PEAKS" repeatedly coursed through my mind. Well, it should definitely be the peak of the spot run. Where would I fish? I decided on Virginia Beach's Little Island Pier in Sandbridge. I knew every spot exiting the Chesapeake Bay would simply *have to* swim past this pier and stretch of beach to migrate south. Besides, there had recently been some outstanding spot runs off this pier just a week or so ago. I now had a plan.

The next morning I loaded all my gear and two light weight rods and reels into my Pathfinder. This trip would also give me a great opportunity to try out a pier cart I had put together for my non-boat retirement fishing. I had taken an off-the-shelf folding plastic and steel cart from West Marine and converted it for the pier by adding a removable rod holder, a knife rack, and an umbrella holder. It was still easy to roll and I was optimistic I could move all my gear, including tackle, bait, food and drink, umbrella, and beach chair, in one single walk out to the pier. Once packed, I left with great anticipation of success!

AFTER LEAVING THE HOUSE, I drove leisurely through some of Virginia Beach's few remaining country back roads. The meandering two-lane road suddenly broke free from its cathedral-like overhanging trees and quickly changed from treed farm areas to the shoreline community of Sandbridge and its main road leading right to the city pier. Sandbridge is truly a "bridge" or connecting strip of barrier sand running from southern Virginia Beach to Corolla, North Carolina. To the east lies nothing but Atlantic Ocean. To the west, behind a narrow strip of sand, is the brackish Back Bay National Wildlife Refuge. Back Bay is a body of mostly landlocked water that is fairly "fresh" in regard to salinity. Prior to the 1930's, saltwater over wash occurred from ocean storms. In this period, dunes were initiated with human assistance, and then Mother Nature took over to insure large enough dunes to prevent further over wash. This action basically secured the bay as a primarily freshwater bay.

This unique bay is situated in a 9000-acre national preserve. Back Bay does, however, have a true opening to saltwater east of Knott's Island where it connects with Currituck Sound. Currituck Sound, in turn, is continuous with Albemarle and Pamlico Sounds, eventually reaching ocean water via the entrance to Oregon Inlet on North Carolina's Outer Banks. Because of this water geography, Back Bay is considered one of the biggest natural estuaries on the East Coast and is a popular fishing destination. It is also considered a watershed. Due to its connection to the ocean, the bay does have a local population of both blue crabs and flounder. Interestingly, the tides within the bay tend to be wind generated. When winds are from the south, water is pushed into the bay causing the tide to "rise." A north wind will create a "falling" tide.

Driving past this area reminded me of a fishing trip to Back Bay when I was stationed in Hampton Roads with the U.S. Navy. My fishing partner and I had rented a small boat from a livery on the bay and set out to catch some of the then highly-touted bass. It turned into one of the shortest fishing trips I have ever taken.

11

After heading out into the bay and dropping our lines in, I remember seeing a huge commotion on the surface of the water approaching our boat. As we both looked at it, we witnessed a large frog swimming full speed and then vaulting out of the water, going airborne as he attempted to jump into our boat. Before the frog had a chance to land, a snake followed right behind him, vaulted out of the water, went over the starboard side of our boat, and snared the frog in mid-air with his now wide open white mouth and fangs. Just as quickly as he grabbed and swallowed the frog, the snake's momentum carried all six feet of him clear across our open twelve-foot boat and back into the water on the other side. The snake then swam off in a lazy S pattern as we watched in disbelief.

"Greg, did you see that?"

"You're damn right I saw that!"

We were both visibly shaken.

"From the white mouth, I'd say it was a water moccasin, Mike."

"I think we've had enough fishing. Let's get the hell out of here before we become bait."

We motored back to the boat ramp in record time and beat a hasty retreat from Back Bay. The bay was beautiful, but oh, was it ever primitive. With this harrowing memory, I concluded my leisurely drive to the pier at Sandbridge, just adjacent to Back Bay.

When I arrived at the pier, I was pleasantly surprised that even with all my gear loaded in it, I could still easily manage to push my new pier cart up the bumpy sloping wooden incline leading to the pier entrance. Once at the gate, I discovered an even more welcomed surprise. No pier attendant and no admission charge for fishing! The city had been gracious enough to leave the pier open for fall striper fishermen even though the summer tourist season was done. Fine with me.

After picking my ideal spot (no fish pun intended) and setting up my beach umbrella and folding chair, I baited up and tossed my double hook bottom rig in with its scent laden bloodworms. They were really expensive—nine dollars for ten worms, a true gourmet bait. The little suckers needed to start earning their expensive keep about now!

It was time to sprawl back in the chair and check out the scene. As it was a weekday, there were only five other fishermen on the pier, a father and son pair and three individual anglers. I started to eat my sandwich and observe the action. As idyllic as the day was, there did not seem to be any fishing action. Some of the people were using squid as bait, but even that didn't seem to make a difference. Squid is such good universal saltwater bait that if they were not catching *anything*, fishing had to be really bad. Further inspection revealed a squadron of pelicans flying low over the water. The surfers I had enjoyed watching during my last August pier visit were noticeably absent now that school was open. What a shame. A perfect day for fishing, but no one told the fish. Oh well, I decided to relax in the warmth of the sun and see what more the morning might bring.

SOMETIME AFTER FINISHING my food and almost dozing off, I looked around the pier and decided to talk to the other anglers. Some had been there quite a while and none had caught any spot. In fact they had caught absolutely nothing. No skates, no sharks, no mullet. Nothing! What to do for the rest of the day suddenly became clear. I said to myself, *Michael, if you move quickly, you can pack up your gear, drive back to Virginia Beach, and arrive just in time to fish the outgoing tide at Rudee Inlet.* This was another known spot haven in the fall. If nothing was biting there, I would pack up again and go home.

When I got to Rudee Inlet there were only a few people fishing, and they said they had caught nothing so far. At least it wasn't any worse than where I had just been. In fact, one man said he had been there for the last twelve hours and lamented his bad luck, saying he was about to pack up and leave. Since I already had most of my nice fresh expensive unused worms left, I decided I would at least wet a line and try it.

Fishing from the Rudee Inlet shore there are three challenges an angler must overcome before he can even think about fishing successfully. One is the constant parade of boats through the inlet forcing the angler to continually reel in to avoid having his line cut by propellers of passing boats. Not a real problem on this fall weekday afternoon. Most boats were in port and the few that had gone out were still out for the afternoon chasing stripers. The second major challenge was to keep reeling steadily as the line approached the rocks or risk becoming hung up with a subsequent loss of gear and fish. These same large rocks also presented a unique concern for safety, balance, and dexterity as they sloped more severely as they approached the water. As a survivor of two neck and two back spinal surgeries, it was particularly imperative for me to be extra careful.

Knowing this venture would be a light tackle approach, I carried only my rod, a bucket with a small amount of ice, and a homemade bait board as I walked part way up the canal bank on the north side of the inlet. My strategy was to cast halfway across the inlet to the deeper navigable water and slowly work my rig toward the shallow side edge near me. On my second cast, as soon as my bloodworms worked their way to shallower water, I started to feel some pulls on the line. Yea! Maybe I could just catch a few pigfish or even a skate to avoid getting skunked for the day.

Annoyingly, something was biting well but not getting hooked and doing a good job of cleaning my worms off the hook. Finally I put on larger bloodworm pieces and switched to larger #4 Eagle Claw hooks. This resulted in an immediate solid hookup. When I reeled in and played the fish over the rocks, it appeared to be a nice-sized croaker so I threw it in the bucket without too much thought. After I quickly caught two more similar fish, the man who had started to pack up to leave came over and asked me about my bait and rig. He decided to stay and fish and was quickly hooked up in the same school. The man was now smiling and even broke into a little song and dance. "Fish sandwich, fish sandwich, I'm gonna have a fish sandwich tonight!" I was glad he was so elated. I would be too if I'd been there the last twelve hours and had caught nothing.

Another nice retired gentleman came by complaining that he had driven to the inlet to fish but had forgotten his rod. He took one look at the fish we were catching and told us he was going straight home and would be right back with his rod. Sure enough, he was back in fifteen minutes and jumped in on the action. In the meantime, I had been steadily filling the bucket with fish, many of which were turning out to be good-sized spot. Frequently we would pull them up two at a time. Now this was worth the drive back from Sandbridge! This was not just fishing, this was CATCHING! This whole flurry of intense action lasted around two hours and then stopped as quickly as it had started as the outgoing tide started to slow.

The day was now made. I had fish. I had dinner. I had redeemed myself. It was late afternoon and I wanted to meet Nancy for dinner, so I packed up my gear, bid farewell to my two jetty buddies, and lugged my now-heavy fish bucket back to the car. It was only four-thirty when I looked at my watch. It would be dark in half an hour, but I also knew that the local tackle shop, Princess Anne Distributing, would still be open. I said to myself, *Just for laughs, why don't I take the spot by the tackle shop and see if any of them come close to citation weight?* I really didn't think any of them would make the one pound cut off for the Virginia Saltwater Fishing Tournament, but I wanted to see how close I might have come.

When I walked into the shop, I asked Josh Anderson if he could weigh one of the spot for me. I fumbled and probed in the ice cold bucket for a minute and handed him one for the scale. "Here's one of the bigger ones from today."

"One pound even."

"Are you certain, Josh?"

"Go ahead and look at it yourself. It's right on one pound."

"You know, I think there might be an even bigger one in the bucket."

After another brutal cold water hand immersion I handed him another spot.

"Let's see, this one goes one pound, two ounces."

I was completely taken by surprise. The initial disappointment of the fishing trip had magically turned into two spot citations in one day!

I WAS SO ELATED that I called Nancy to tell her, and she was equally excited for me. I must have caught the end of the annual spot migration as they were schooling to leave Rudee Inlet for the season. It was classic—for once I had been at the right place at the right time with the right bait and it all came together.

As the November sun set and I drove home, I knew that although I would not receive my state citation plaque until the spring, I would be able to bask in the warmth and enjoyment of this fishing trip all winter long. This would most definitely keep me going until fishing weather returned in the spring. Truly a *double back double citation day* to remember!

Captain's Tip: Do fish peaks and don't ever give up. When you are not catching, it can only get better! Also, small hooks can always catch a large fish; however, the reverse is not always true. Several artificial baits have been perfected to the point where they can easily replace bloodworms making your fishing easier, less troublesome, and more economical.

Captain's Note: The state of Virginia sponsors an annual saltwater fishing tournament that is open to anglers of all ages, including both residents and non-residents. Fish entered in the contest that meet minimum weight requirements within a species are awarded free handsome, colorful wall plaques or "citations." The person who catches the largest fish in each of the eligible species receives an actual trophy. Additionally, anglers who capture multiple citations in a variety of species can qualify as "Expert" or "Master" anglers. There is also a special award category for "Junior" anglers who are fifteen years of age and younger. Anyone seeking additional information about this program can contact the Virginia Saltwater Fishing Tournament directly:

Virginia Saltwater Fishing Tournament
Suite 102, Hauser Bldg.
968 Oriole Drive, South
Virginia Beach, Virginia 23451

Tel. No: (757) 491-5160
Fax No: (757) 491-5172
E-mail: mrcswt@visi.net

3

A Wreck and Its Treasure

A NUMBER OF YEARS ago my nephew and niece, Jason and Gwen Schoenborn, came to visit my wife and me in Virginia Beach. Since they rarely had an opportunity to visit Virginia Beach, we planned several activities we thought they might enjoy. During their visit we decided on a trip to Busch Gardens and an offshore fishing trip with their "Uncle Mike." As a sixteen-year-old young man and fourteen-year-old young lady, they were excited to be able to be boating on the Atlantic Ocean since they lived in landlocked Syracuse, New York.

Not knowing their tolerance for "mal de mer," I carefully chose a fair weather, low wind forecast day in August. My wife packed our lunches and the three of us set out at daybreak in my twenty-four foot Sea Ray, *Drifter II,* to attempt some shark fishing in Virginia Beach's warm coastal waters.

As it was a beautiful flat calm day, we were able to leave Lynnhaven Inlet and arrive at the red "2V" buoy off Virginia Beach in about forty-five minutes. The "2V" buoy marks the wreck of the World War II ship *Tiger* that now rests on the bottom twelve miles southeast of Rudee Inlet and ten miles due east of Sandbridge. The *Tiger* was a 5707 ton nautical tanker that was torpedoed and sunk in sixty feet of water on April 3, 1942, by a German U-boat. The wreck is marked by lighted bell buoy "2V." Hence, local fishermen know it simply as the "2V" buoy. It is also a popular destination for head-boats as well as dive boats filled with tourists and locals. The wreck is comprised of several pieces of the ship normally teeming with sea bass, flounder, Spanish mackerel, bluefish and amberjack spring through fall. My plan upon arrival was to hunt for something larger that also was known to occasionally inhabit this area—brown sharks.

ONCE ANCHORED, I rigged up two Penn Senator rod and reel combos, a 6/0 and 9/0, both with fifteen-foot nylon covered wire cable leaders and double hook shark rigs. Our starting baits were blue-fish and tuna heads obtained from mates in the charter fleet at Rudee Inlet. The heads were fresh discards from the cleaning of the prior day's catch. My niece, Gwen, went up to the bow to work on her tan while Jason and I rigged the fish heads. By doing so, Gwen cleverly managed to avoid the aromatic and offensive loading of the chum bucket! Our chum consisted of chunks of frozen ground fish scraps placed in a plastic five-gallon bucket drilled full of one-inch holes which allowed the scraps to slowly float out in the current. In addition to the baits, this oily slick, I hoped, would be the key to our success. Now it was time to sit back, enjoy the beautiful sunny weather, and wait for the tell-tale dipping of one of the rod tips that would be our first sign of a pick up for one of the baits. Jason's assigned job was to watch the balloon attached to the float rig on the 6/0 since the 9/0 had been sent straight to the bottom in sixty feet of water.

No other boats were present on this week day as we had left quite early to get started on our fishing, and it was great having the entire wreck to ourselves. Finally, after a long hour and a half, we started catching some two to three-foot long sandbar sharks that were hardly any sport on the large rods and reels we were using. As these were the first sharks Jason had ever seen up close, he was ecstatic. Although I did not express the thought to my nephew, I was disappointed that a larger shark had not appeared from the depths. I let Jason reel the sharks up to the boat where I unhooked them, tagged them, and then released them back into the ocean. Jason was fascinated to learn about the National Marine Fisheries tagging program. Each waterproof tag contains a capsule with a note in five languages asking the angler to report specific data upon capture. Items to be reported include species, fork length, and specific location by GPS numbers. This re-search data is compiled and used by Marine Fisheries to study growth rates and migration patterns for each species of shark. With luck, data from the tagged fish will eventually be recovered at the next capture of the shark.

"The next small shark we catch is going back in the water as bait," I said after we caught several more brown sharks.

My nephew looked at me like I was crazy. "Are you kidding?" he said.

"No, Jason," I answered. "I'm quite serious. Maybe we can in-terest something bigger if we use a good-sized live bait."

Within fifteen minutes we had yet another two-foot-plus brown shark reeled up to the boat. I made Jason hold the small shark down to deter his thrashing as the shark tried everything possible to free himself. I removed the large hook from his mouth and used the two hooks from the 9/0 rig to bridle him as a live bait. He would now be able to swim freely but with a somewhat impeded motion and speed due to the weight of the double-hook rig and attached cable leader. With any luck that would allow the shark to broadcast "injured fish" vibrations into the surrounding water. Then I asked my nephew to hold his hand on the reel spool while I lowered our bait shark back into the water. Jason said that this bait was bigger than any fish he had ever seen or caught in fresh water in New York. I told him to remember that he was now fishing in the Atlantic Ocean, and there were many huge fish prowling these waters. Maybe he would get lucky this day and catch one of them.

Someone must have heard my wish.

"Uncle Mike, I think the line is moving off a lot quicker now," he suddenly said as he held his fingers on the reel spool to prevent an over run as our new bait swam slowly toward the bottom.

As I looked at the spool, I could see the bait shark was running line off the reel at a rapid rate. It appeared that the bait was swimming scared and was about to be picked up by something much bigger.

I rushed to grab a gimbal belt and my fighting harness and hurriedly prepared Jason for an anticipated battle.

"Continue to keep your hand on the spool and don't let it backlash!" I shouted. By now the clicker on the 9/0 was starting to sound off with rapid staccato noise as something took off on a run with our shark bait!

"What do I do next?" Jason yelled excitedly.

"Just point the rod at the disappearing line in the water, throw the reel in gear, reel until the line comes tight, and then strike the fish like I showed you when we set up this morning."

Jason did exactly that and then struck hard again two more times. By now we had interrupted Gwen's sunbathing and she rushed to the stern of the boat. Whatever had picked up our shark bait rapidly ran off about two hundred yards of 80-pound test Dacron line. I told Jason to just hold on and do nothing while the fish continued to run. Then I coached him on what to do once the initial run was over.

"Pump and reel! Pump and reel!"

Jason was young and strong, and I figured he should be able to win this battle if he followed my instructions. For the next hour and a half, battle he did. It was a constant back and forth between Jason and the fish. To Jason's advantage was the homemade fighting chair mounted on a swivel base in the middle of the cockpit. This allowed him to brace his legs against the gunwales so he didn't have to rely strictly on his back and arms to defeat the fish. I also encouraged him to periodically rest his arms by letting the fighting harness take the strain of the rod and the fish while he shook out the stiffness from his biceps and forearms.

EVER SO SLOWLY, Jason's fish finally started to rise toward the surface. When it eventually showed itself, Jason got a renewed burst of energy. My nephew had hooked a *huge*, angry dusky shark! After he got over the initial shock of seeing how large the shark was, I told him he had to fight even harder and smarter because he had hooked one of the most difficult fish to boat. Dusky sharks are famous for spreading their large pectoral fins out and using them to exert tremendous force against the water and the angler in their effort to escape capture. Jason would definitely have to work harder for us to be able to ever get control of the leader. After a long arduous struggle and the fish forcing Jason to walk around the boat numerous times, I was finally able to reach and grab the leader. Each time I tried to hold onto the leader, the fish took off like a freight train and surged away from the boat.

"Jason, you need to tire him out a little more, so I can hold onto the leader. Gwen, you need to help me pull on the leader once I grab it again."

With her extra weight, I thought we might have a chance to gain control.

As tired as he was, Jason took my urgings to heart. He dug down deep into his reserve strength and proceeded to ever so slowly continue to crank his hard-earned line back on the reel. With each successive reeling, the fish ran off again to stop a little closer to the boat. As the dusky shark approached the boat on Jason's ninth attempt at capture, the great fish seemed to be turning on his side.

"Aha, now *we* are about to be in charge for a change," I announced for my nephew and niece to hear. As we had rehearsed earlier, I laid the slip loop circle of my now open tail rope on the deck.

"Jason, stand inside the tail rope so I can work it over you and the rod and then over the fish."

He held still as directed while I quickly slid the half-inch nylon rope up and over his body, down the length of the rod, and over the leader until it reached the tip of the shark's snout. For the moment, the dusky shark was quietly cooperating in the water as Gwen held tightly to the cable leader with leather gloves. Next I grabbed the handle of my scrub brush and leaned over the gunwale to carefully work the rope over the fish's body. The rope was slightly hung on the tip of the dorsal fin. No problem, a quick wrist flick of the brush handle flipped the line over the tip and on to the shark's back. As I poked the rope toward the end of the shark's body and the front of its great tail, I slid sideways to a position just in front of the port stern cleat.

Everything looked right with the fish and the tail rope, so I jerked the rope hard closing it on the shark's tail while swiftly pulling the loose end of the rope down and around the bottom of the cleat finishing with one complete turn on the cleat. At the same time, I leaned back on the rope with my full body weight to restrain the shark which had just gone berserk.

"Leave the rod in its holder and help me hold the tail rope!" I instructed. "Gwen, come over and grab the rope with us too until this shark settles down."

Gwen didn't hesitate to help even though the shark was flailing and thrashing his tail against the side of the boat.

After almost ten minutes with the three of us holding the rope, the fish was calm enough so I could take additional wraps around the cleat to better secure the fish. With each new wrap, I asked Jason to help me lift the shark's tail higher and higher out of the water until the fish could no longer create any havoc with us or the boat. Following this, we secured several more tail ropes and left the rod in the forward rod holder with minimal drag. This provided us with a second attachment to the shark. The rod, leader, and hook afforded us a necessary safety measure in case the shark tried to work his way loose during the ride to shore.

I then took stock of my niece and nephew before we headed back to port. Jason was pretty tired but happy and elated over his first ever saltwater catch. Gwen seemed to have the *I really don't believe what I just saw my brother catch* look on her face. I could tell they were both quite excited about how the day had turned out. Then I told them to grab a cold drink because it was going to be a long, slow ride to Lynnhaven Inlet. Even with the special fish handling roller on my stern, this shark was just too big and heavy for the three of us to winch into the boat with the come-a-long I had on board.

It was still a pretty nice day as I fired up the Mercruiser and started idling on a course toward Cape Henry at about three and a half knots. I made sure Jason and Gwen stayed hydrated with drinks, and the three of us tried to stay under the canvas top to avoid baking in the afternoon August sun. I also called my wife on the VHF radio to let her know that we were heading in and that Jason had worked very hard to catch a splendid dusky shark. He had had an amazing introduction to the joys and rigors of saltwater angling in the ocean, and I was really proud of him.

About an hour and a half later, as I steered *Drifter* under the Lynnhaven Bridge and turned left, I looked at the beach and there was Craig Paige standing on the shore to greet us and give a nice thumbs up once he saw what we were towing in. When we pulled up to the dock, both Nancy and Craig were there to greet us. After tying up, the guys at Lynnhaven Marine came over with the huge fork lift they normally used to launch boats and picked up our shark for the weighing process. When the dusky shark was put on the scale it weighed in at 439 pounds! An awesome catch for a sixteen-year-old on his first ocean fishing adventure! He and his sister slept quite soundly that night.

A FEW DAYS LATER, my wife and I packed my niece and nephew off for the return trip to Syracuse, New York, complete with memories of Busch Gardens and ocean angling that should last them both a lifetime. As their uncle, I thoroughly enjoyed sharing the best that Virginia Beach angling could offer them.

Captain's Tip: When taking young anglers fishing, always emphasize safety procedures above all and never underestimate what a teenager can accomplish with proper instruction and guidance. When wiring a large fish, particularly a shark, always wear a pair of leather gloves and *never* wrap the leader around your hands. You should always be prepared to release the leader instantly should the fish run from the boat.

4

A Mighty Strange Flounder

I HAD OWNED my twenty-four foot Sea Ray walk-a-round cuddy cabin fisherman for only a few months, but I was already enjoying running the boat as much as fishing from it. One hot, humid, steamy July day, Louis Ford and I had arranged to go flounder fishing in the Chesapeake Bay.

Louis was and still is a personable and intelligent young man, and we had become friends through our shared interest in shark fishing and the Virginia Beach Sharkers. I had spent some time showing him the fine points of making up shark fishing hook and leader rigs, and the two of us hit it off from day one. Louis had a highly unusual job working for Lifenet, a local organ transplant procurement company. There would never be a dull conversation when discussing daily work stories with Louis!

On the day we left on our fishing trip the bay was like a mirror, and *Drifter II* quickly sped across the eleven miles from Lynnhaven Inlet to my "honey hole" at the "R-12" channel buoy. We would be fishing the northern edge of the Baltimore shipping channel, not far from the Chesapeake Bay Bridge Tunnel. This location had regularly proven itself to be a consistent producer of good-sized flounder. We just needed to time the tide right and use enough lead to firmly hold bottom in the usually wicked tidal current. The channel edge is a gently sloping ledge that runs from the sixty-foot deep water of the channel to the twenty-five foot shoal behind the fourth rock island of the Chesapeake Bay Bridge Tunnel. This bottom structure, coupled with a moving tide, is equivalent to ringing a dinner bell for any hungry flounder. I always envisioned scores of minnows and small crabs sweeping over this slope while voracious flounders eyed them from below, their eyes sticking out from their buried positions in the sand as they camouflaged themselves and faced into the current prior to pouncing on a passing meal.

With high hopes that all of these factors would work to our advantage, I turned off the engine. Louis and I quickly baited up before beginning our first drift of the day for flounder. Once we had rigged "Old Salt" fluke rigs tipped with fat bull gudgeon minnows and strips of squid, I restarted the engine and idled up to the "R-12" channel buoy. Both of us began to slowly lower our five-ounce lead-weighted rigs the nearly fifty feet to the soft sand bottom of the bay. Once they thumped on the bottom, we both let out another seventy-five feet of line to give enough scope to hold bottom in the still accelerating current. We were fishing the early phase of an incoming tide. Each of us placed our rods in a port side gunwale rod holder and then rigged up a second rod and reel. We would hold the second rods and reels and fish them actively while the first two rigs worked their magic from the boat motion. For the "dead" rods, all we had to do was watch the rod tips for that telltale tap of a flounder biting the end of our bait. That would be a pronounced downward dip of the rod tip as opposed to the regular gentle bouncing of the sinkers on the bottom.

THAT MORNING THE BITES were immediate and steady. It was going to be a good day! We began catching flounder at a predictable but not overwhelming pace. None were very large, however, with half of them regaining their freedom as undersized throwbacks, being smaller than the thirteen-inch limit required that year in Virginia.

About an hour into the morning's fishing, the rod I was holding transmitted up its length what I perceived to be the sharp yet very weak *tap, tap, tap* of a small flounder biting. I decided to give him a few moments to try and get the bait fully into his mouth if he could. Suddenly the tapping stopped, and my entire line started to slowly and steadily move off at a tangent from the boat. I quickly made a mental note that we were right near the "R-12" buoy on the channel edge. I didn't think we had snagged the buoy chain, so I just held on for about thirty seconds. The line on my spinning reel was rapidly disappearing into the bay, so it was now decision time. I decided to clamp down on the reel and attempt to set the hook. The moment I reared back and struck, I knew I had hooked something solid and *very* strong. This was no snag!

My first thought was SHARK. I figured he would either cut me off fast or the 30-pound monofilament line would quickly abrade from the shark's rough skin, freeing the fish. As I applied pressure, the unseen prey started to come up quickly toward the surface of the bay.

"Good," I said loud enough so Louis could hear it. "Let's break this line off so we can both get back to flounder fishing."

"Maybe we should see what you've hooked before you break it off."

While I was playing with my yet-to-be-seen quarry, Louis had expertly reeled in and cleared the other three lines so they would not get tangled or torn up by the shark. He was now anxiously watching me apply pressure to the fish.

For some unknown reason, the shark had not yet abraded or chewed through the line.

"Must be hooked in the corner of the mouth," I remarked to Louis. I continued to play the fish. "Let me put still more pressure on him, and maybe I can get the line to abrade on his skin."

Since we were flounder fishing that day, and I had routinely been catching three, four, and five-hundred pound sharks offshore, I was not particularly interested in wasting the morning playing with a small bay shark. Louis just watched patiently and got out a National Marine Fisheries shark tag in case we got the fish up to the boat.

About five minutes into the battle, a funny thing happened. The fish surfaced and started to circle the boat repeatedly. I finally got a good look at the fish.

"This fish has no large dorsal fin. I don't think it's a shark," I excitedly exclaimed.

"You're right! That is no shark." Louis just stared at the fish which was about fifty yards away, still circling the boat. Now I was shouting. "Louis, I believe it's a large cobia!"

We both looked at each other and were mutually astounded by what we saw.

"Now that I know what we are dealing with, I think I'll lighten up on the pressure as a 2/0 'Old Salt' fluke rig hook is the only thing connecting me to this fish and I don't want to lose it."

Then the battle truly began. The cobia circled the boat close to sixteen times as I continuously walked around the cuddy cabin and repeatedly returned to the cockpit. All the while I kept trying to tire the fish by applying more and more pressure without straightening the relatively miniscule hook that was connecting the two of us. A lifetime of angling experience proved invaluable as I continued to fight the cobia with a calculated mix of force and patience. *Please let this hook hold until I can boat this fish!* I kept saying to myself.

Ever so slowly the circles in which the fish was swimming began to grow tighter. We had now drifted directly into the middle of the Baltimore shipping channel. Louis was aware of this and was doing a great job watching for freighters that could suddenly appear on the horizon. After forty minutes the cobia was very close to the boat and appeared to be finally tiring. At some point I was going to have to increase the pressure enough to get the fish close to the boat. I also was aware that cobia have a well-earned and fabled history of tearing up boats and anglers if landed before they are sufficiently fatigued.

I was dreading the pending end game, constantly having a mental picture of that very small 2/0 "Old Salt" hook barely holding me to this heavy fish. *Oh well*, I thought. *No guts, no glory.*

"Louis, it is now the moment of truth. I plan to slightly increase the pressure and lead this cobia to the boat so you can net him. I don't know if we'll get more than one shot at boating this fish because he's barely hooked."

I now needed to rely on Louis to dip the net completely in the water before I pulled the cobia to it. This was the teamwork we needed so we wouldn't spook the fish and cause him to run. Louis knew exactly what to do. He submerged the net, allowing me to slowly direct the now worn-out cobia into the net. Once the fish was in the net, he lifted the handle vertically, blocking any possible path of escape for the cobia.

"Now, let's get this fish in the boat!" I yelled.

Using the net, Louis and I together hoisted the heavy fish into the boat where the cobia lay motionless on the deck in the net. The only movement visible was the rise and fall of his pectoral area as he breathed.

I then had another decision to make. Visual inspection quickly determined that this was almost definitely a citation fish under the Virginia Saltwater Fishing Tournament guidelines. I thought about the pros and cons of killing the fish and eating him. It was a decision quickly made.

"Louis, let's pack up the gear and go back to the dock to weigh this fish for a possible citation, okay?"

Together we again lifted the fish and, as best we could, placed him in the only cooler on board. He did not come close to fitting in the fifty-six quart Igloo cooler we had brought for our flounder.

AS I SPED toward the inlet, I glanced back at the fish and decided he looked ridiculous. Only about half of him fit in the cooler. His tail and rear body section extended beyond the cooler and its top. He also now had a very damp fishing towel draped over the end sticking out. This was to minimize dehydration and weight loss from sun exposure during our trip in. I had fought too long and too hard to lose a prize citation to Virginia heat and humidity!

Once we were idling inside the inlet, I contacted the marine operator who patched me through from my VHF radio to my wife, Nancy, on the home phone. (These were pre-cell phone days.) I asked her to meet us at the dock with a camera and a much larger cooler. I intended to take pictures, weigh the fish, and send the fish home on ice with Nancy pending a later cleaning. Then Louis and I could run back out to the bay to resume the flounder fishing we had just begun two hours before.

All went as planned. Nancy drove right to the dry storage marina and took some great pictures. When the fish was finally placed on the scale, it weighed in at fifty-one pounds and eight ounces. This was a clear citation, and our speed and care in the heat probably preserved its qualifying weight. I now felt somewhat better about removing such a magnificent fish from the estuary. I not only had the citation but also knew it would provide many good meals for Louis and me.

As Louis and I sped back out to our flounder spot, we had already had a great day fishing even if we never caught another flounder for the day. I was thankful that the small 2/0 "Old Salt" fluke hook held as long as it did, enabling the opportunity for a great catch. Louis and I were also glad that when we returned to the Chesapeake Bay Bridge Tunnel for more fishing, the flounder were still biting.

In retrospect, I believe the cobia probably ate the small flounder I had hooked, leading to his ultimate demise. It is truly ironic how many crazy things can happen when fishing, especially the occurrence of situations that are highly unexpected. This is what makes saltwater angling so exciting and unpredictable and why I love it so much. This is one fishing trip both Louis and I will vividly remember forever.

Captain's tip: Be prepared for the unexpected. Always carry a large enough landing net and cooler no matter what you are fishing for. Elephants *do* eat peanuts! Cobia are big, strong, potentially boat-wrecking fish—do not bring one aboard until it is completely tired out and then do so with great caution.

Captain's Eco Note: Much effort is going into tagging flounder along our East Coast. The data from these fish are invaluable in monitoring the resource as information is gathered on migration patterns and growth rates. If a tagged fish is caught, I encourage every angler to measure it, record the length and tag number, release the fish, and call in the tag information. The Virginia Saltwater Fishing Tournament program rewards all anglers who capture tagged fish with their choice of a free cap, shirt, or pin.

5

Mano, Ahi, and A'u

MY WIFE AND I were fortunate enough to both be teaching in public schools where we had two months free to travel each summer. Since I had gone to sea for six months with the U.S. Navy immediately after getting married ten years earlier, we both felt like we owed ourselves a long overdue honeymoon. We had always wanted to go to Hawaii, so in 1981, for our tenth anniversary, we made the plane and hotel reservations to visit the various islands.

I was already heavily involved in East Coast shark fishing at this time, and I had heard there were some superb oceanic white tip, tiger, and great white sharks frequenting the deep Pacific waters adjacent to Hawaii. In addition to the necessary tropical clothing, I carefully packed a pair of my hand-tied 16/0 twisted number nineteen wire shark rigs in a heavy duty plastic zippered bag. These were buried in the middle of my suitcase and, except for the airport metal detector test, forgotten about until we unpacked on Oahu, the first island of our month-long vacation.

After the usual sightseeing, luaus, and Don Ho on Oahu, we flew to Maui and I booked a group charter on an old Chris Craft that had been converted for sport fishing. There were five other people on board, and we were all assigned the obligatory "turn" or "hour" to own the rods in case a fish hit during our turn. This was a very fair system, although leaving most of the anglers as spectators most of the time. As our day unfolded, there was to be only one fish that would hit and, as the odds had it, it was not to be my turn on the rod. Another young man had the pleasure of cranking in a thirty-five pound wahoo which had pounced on one of the lures with colorful artificial skirts that we were dragging behind in our wake. This was my first fishing experience in Hawaii, and I simply enjoyed the weather, the sea breeze, and the beauty of the mountainous shore and the Pacific Ocean.

As we continued our island hopping through Hawaii, we eventually got to the "big island" or the one called Hawaii. This was where I was determined to do some shark fishing. The day after our arrival, Nancy and I drove down to Honokohau Harbor, which is on the lee side or Kona Coast of Hawaii. After we parked on a lava bed parking lot, I began to walk the docks looking for a captain I could convince to take me shark fishing. Convince turned out to be an understatement. Almost all of the boats were set up strictly for marlin and tuna fishing, and the captains I initially spoke with had no interest in taking a client out for sharks. I was discouraged thinking I might not get a shark charter in Hawaii. I later learned that it is Hawaiian lore that ancestral spirits reside in current day sharks, and most captains were reluctant to pursue them.

Just as Nancy and I were about to drive away from Honokohau harbor, I passed a beautifully kept Jersey sport fishing boat that was just being cleaned up from a day of fishing. The name on the transom read *Lei Aloha*. I said hello to the mate in the cockpit who had a hose in his hand, and he invited Nancy and me to come on board and talk to him. The mate was Randy Parker. Once he found out that I was interested in a charter, he called Captain Jim Hunter up on deck to talk to us. Jim seemed somewhat receptive to my idea about shark fishing, but he was not overly excited about it. After conversing for a while, he made me an offer.

"Let's do this, if you are agreeable. We'll fish for sharks in the morning and if we have not had any success by noon, we'll troll for marlin and tuna. I just don't want to take you on a charter and not have you catch anything."

By now, I was finally excited! After my experience on Maui, I decided to take the charter out by myself to increase my odds of getting a prize fish. Plus Captain Hunter was actually agreeable to my fishing for sharks with his rods and reels and my leaders. Nancy and I then gave him a required deposit and told him I'd see him in the morning on the next day. Nancy remembers that all I could talk about that night at dinner was what a great time I was going to have on the charter.

THE NEXT MORNING I rose for an early breakfast in the hotel and then drove our rental car to the harbor where the *Lei Aloha*, Jim Hunter's Jersey, was moored. Randy came out first and helped me board across a narrow brow that extended from the stern to the parking lot bulkhead.

Once my gear was stowed, Jim Hunter fired up the twin diesels and Randy freed the boat from the bow, stern, and spring lines. I asked him how long I could relax before we would begin fishing. His reply shocked me.

"Oh, about five minutes."

I looked at him incredulously as it was well over an hour and a half run to get to any real deep water off the Virginia coast. With each of the Hawaiian Islands being the result of violent volcanic upheaval in mid-ocean, we would be in deep water almost as soon as we cleared the harbor entrance.

True to his word, within about five minutes we were drifting just off shore and Randy had rigged up one of my terminal shark rigs on an 80-pound class Penn rod and 10/0 reel. I was impressed by the beauty of the boat's rods. They were truly the most exceptional rods I had ever seen. Each of the rods on the boat had gorgeous colorful matching wraps in orange, brown, yellow, and gold. This same color motif perfectly matched the way the boat's name *Lei Aloha* had been done in multi-color letters across the transom. Everything here was first class, and I hoped the obvious attention to detail would also translate into a great day of fishing.

I LOOKED around the cockpit and there was a huge brown plastic trash barrel lashed in place in the port corner.

"Randy, what is that for?"

"That is where I am going to put the shark bait you are about to catch."

As soon as he said that, he handed me one of the smaller rods that had been baited with a small strip of tuna belly and a single hook and directed me to start dropping the bait into the depths until he told me to stop.

Meanwhile, Jim Hunter was busy on the fly bridge studying his depth finder. "Mike, I'm beginning to mark amberjack all over the top of this reef, which is about 160 feet below us. As soon as you get in the strike zone, I'll ask you to come out of free spool and lock the reel in drag."

Jim Hunter never had to tell me to throw the lever, because about two minutes later a bruiser of an amberjack grabbed the bait and took off with it. After locking down on him, it took me a good fifteen minutes to wear him down enough to crank him all the way up to the boat.

"How's that for a warm-up drill?" Randy shouted.

Randy grabbed the monofilament line and deftly gaffed the big amberjack all with one smooth motion. Jim assisted him in dragging the amberjack over the gunwale and into the trash barrel head first!

Within moments, Jim was back on the fly bridge and heading off to a special area he thought might hold some white tip or tiger sharks. At the same time, Randy began to fillet a side of fresh amberjack that we would use for bait. Once the bait was filleted, I asked Randy to let me position it exactly where I wanted on my hook rig. Then it was off to drifting again while Randy rigged a duplicate bait from the other side of the amberjack. One rig was suspended about two-hundred feet below the boat while the second one drifted off a float rig about thirty feet below the surface. The only thing we did not have going for us was some fresh chum, which apparently was not customarily used in Hawaiian game fishing. At least we had two *very* fresh baits at work for us.

FOR THREE HOURS of the morning we drifted on the placid Pacific in anticipation of the shark bite that never came. Randy, Jim, and I talked fishing the entire time. I was really disappointed that we had absolutely no takers on these two very fresh baits. I kept thinking that the lack of chum was making the difference in our luck.

At exactly 11:30 A.M., Captain Jim was ready to begin his hunt for tuna and marlin.

"Okay Randy, lines in. Well, Mike, we've done it your way all morning, now it's time for my way." Almost before he was done talking, Randy had finished cranking in the last of the two shark leaders and baits. Once he removed the baits, he handed me both of my terminal rigs, which he had sprayed clean with fresh water. My disappointment with Hawaiian shark fishing would soon be replaced by enthusiasm for marlin fishing.

"I guess I'll have to wait until I'm home in Virginia to put these two rigs back in use again."

As Randy rigged the two beautiful 10/0 Penn outfits for marlin fishing, I studied what he was doing for future knowledge. He had taken some 130-pound Dacron line and used it to make a short loop or bridle with a rigging needle on the end. To this he would attach some soon-to-be-caught swimming baits on 9/0 hooks. He explained that the hook would never physically be impaled in the bait in any way. The Dacron would simply be carefully run through the bait's eye sockets and then both sides of the loop would be twisted tight until the J hook rode comfortably on the bait's "nose" in what he described as a towing bridle. Randy said this arrangement would enable the bait to have maximum capacity to swim naturally while also insuring that the hook was completely free to penetrate the marlin's hard mouth once swallowed. It all made sense to me.

While Randy completed rigging these two bridles, Jim started pointing off the starboard side and yelling.

"Aku, Randy, Aku!"

I had no idea what he was yelling, but was about to find out. Randy jumped up from his rigging chores and quickly grabbed a very lightweight Penn 20-pound trolling rod which only had 15-pound test spooled on it with a very small artificial blue jig resembling a three-inch baitfish. This jig was quickly streamed astern of the boat, and Randy began to rapidly raise and lower the rod tip to work the jig. Captain Jim continued to point and yell.

"Aku, Aku, Randy, go get 'em!"

Suddenly the clicker on Randy's lightweight rod started to scream as the unknown quarry took off with the jig. Once the fish was hooked, Randy explained to me that the Aku they were now after were actually skipjack tuna, common to Hawaiian waters and one of the marlin's favorite live bait treats. With slow deliberation, Randy gradually worked his Aku closer and closer to the boat. Once it was off the stern, Jim ran down the ladder from the fly bridge and netted the fish for him. Jim then carefully removed the fish from the net, placing a damp towel over its eyes while simultaneously turning the fish upside down. This calmed it so Randy could put the rigging needle through its eye socket and prepare it on the hook as a live bait. Once this was done, the fish swam in the live well while we resumed trolling in order to snare another skipjack tuna to use on the second trolling rig. As we were surrounded by small schools of Aku, Randy hooked up another tuna within seconds after repeating his rod jigging routine. Resorting to the use of such light line was a trick I would remember years later when finding Spanish mackerel hits hard to come by off Cape Henry on the East Coast.

Both of the newly rigged skipjacks were deftly returned to resume swimming in the Pacific Ocean. Each of the large bent-butt Penn 10/0 outfits sat in opposing corner rod holders of the cockpit. The one on the port side was maybe fifty feet off the transom with the bait swimming just beyond the boat's third wave in the wake. The starboard side rig wound up being placed about three hundred feet from the boat, swimming at a slightly deeper depth. Both baits were now swimming just below the surface.

Now it was time to relax and watch the baits. The noonday Hawaiian sun was heating up. Even though I was well lathered with sunscreen, I decided to sit on top of the bait prep station, which was sheltered from the direct sun by the large overhang from the boat's flying bridge. Jim slowly idled the *Lei Aloha* ahead while Randy and I watched the baits and the rod tips, while talking about everything from work to life in Hawaii. It was very hot, but the view was extremely picturesque. To my right, less than a half mile away, was the Hawaiian shoreline which quickly rose to a panorama of lush and majestically green covered mountains. If I looked left, I could see the perfectly blue Pacific water, with one or two tropical islands visible in the distance.

I WAS RELAXING but also anxiously waiting for a strike. I can remember that as I perched atop the bait prep station and under the boat's bridge top, I suddenly felt some drops of moisture on my face. I stepped out from under the overhang and looked up to see if it had started to rain. There was not a cloud in the sky anywhere near us. Still confused as more water was pummeling me with droplets on my arms and face, I asked Randy what was going on. After laughing for a moment, he answered my question.

"It's quite simple, but unique to Hawaii. We are fishing on the lee side of the Big Island. When the Pacific trade winds hit the other side of the island they sweep up and over the mountains and volcanoes. They carry moisture laden air and then rush down the lee side of the mountains to the coast, driving the moisture as raindrops in front of them—hence the rain from nowhere."

I was surprised by Randy's explanation of this phenomenon, and then it all made perfect sense why I was being hit with horizontal rain with a bright sun and no clouds to be seen. All in all, the rain was a very light and misty relief from the current heat, and I actually enjoyed the coolness of the droplets.

By one o'clock, the skipjacks were still swimming lazily with no customers. I had been drinking bottled water steadily to stay hydrated in the constant heat and decided to see what was for lunch. As part of the full day charter, a complete deli lunch had been pre-packed for the captain, the mate, and me. As his charter client, Jim told me to help myself to whatever sandwiches I might find in the cooler. To this day I can still remember the wonderful chicken salad sandwiches that had been provided. They had a special delicious taste from walnuts, grapes, and dill and were so good that I think I ate three of them by the end of the day. Two o'clock and lunch came and went without a fish bite. It was also getting hotter and hotter.

I remember looking at my watch at about forty-five minutes after two, thinking that I was about to be skunked when the starboard rod tip began to jerk up and down. Randy noticed it at the same time. "See how that bait is getting real nervous? He's about to be eaten. Don't do anything yet. Just watch the rod and let's see what happens."

In an instant the reel started to scream as line flew off and something headed off with our little finned tuna.

"We'll wait till he stops before we do anything. That's when I know he is actually swallowing the bait."

Sure enough, in about thirty seconds the bait appeared to go still in the water. Captain Jim suddenly pushed the throttles forward and raced the boat ahead to try to set the hook on whatever was devouring our Aku. After about ten seconds, Jim slowed to trolling speed as line began to steadily peel off the 10/0 rod and reel. Randy then motioned me to remove the rod and reel from the gunwale rod holder while he slipped me into a bucket fighting harness and led me back to the boat's fighting chair. I guessed all that waiting was now paying off.

The fish continued to take line. Randy coached me to let him go and not try to reel until the fish stopped running. There were over 1200 yards of 80-pound monofilament on the 10/0 reel, so I was not worried. I had always read that marlin liked to jump when hooked so I kept looking at the area where the line disappeared into the water, but there was no fish to be seen. Randy seemed to know what had eaten the Aku.

"I think you've probably hooked a tuna. A marlin would have shown itself or come up toward the surface by now. He's going to dog it deep for a while, so just hang tough."

I DID HANG TOUGH as I fought hard for every foot of line. It seemed like the fish would take thirty feet and then I would regain twenty feet of line. This see-saw battle went on like this for the better part of a half hour. Finally it seemed as though I was starting to win as I inched the fish closer and closer to the boat. Once I was able to use my legs and back to work him up to the surface and close to the stern, the captain left the boat in slow ahead and scrambled down the bridge ladder to assist Randy in the cockpit.

The two of them obviously had done this end game dozens of times before. Jim Hunter opened the wide transom door and told me to just hold onto the big 80-pound class Penn rod and reel and to slack off my drag slightly. The drag needed to be loosened just in case the fish made a last ditch effort to charge away from the boat. For the next five or ten minutes, all I could see were the backsides of Randy and Jim as they both worked feverishly to secure the fish for me.

"Okay, Randy, I've got one gaff in him good. Secure the line to a cleat and then hand me a second gaff."

Still I could not see the fish as they both blocked any view of the open transom door and the fish.

More directions followed for the mate.

"Now give me a line for a tail rope, Randy."

Once they had gained complete control of the fish, Jim used the lip gaff he had placed in the fish's lower jaw to begin to pull him in through the transom door. "You need to help me pull, Randy; he's really heavy. In fact, let's only pull each time the fish rises up on a swell. That should make it easier for us. Okay, Mike, now you can put the rod in a holder and help us pull this fish all the way in to the boat."

After several swells had helped to lift the fish for easier handling, the three of us were finally able to deposit him safely inside the boat's cockpit. As he landed inside the boat, I was able to see a massive, stout, torpedo-shaped tuna. He had two extremely long fins that were bright yellow, one above his back and one protruding from his lower belly area. Additionally, there were two rows of much smaller yellow fins, one row on his dorsal side and one on his belly or ventral side. He had a large, powerful C-shaped tail and a proud fan-like fin on the front of his back. His upper back was a dark blue color in contrast to the very white coloration of his underside. His large, translucent eye seemed to be staring at us from the deck where he now lay helplessly captured. I had managed to catch a very large and equally beautiful yellow fin tuna!

CAPTAIN JIM EXPLAINED that the fan-like fin on the tuna's back retracted into a groove to allow him to swim even faster when necessary. I thought that was a pretty amazing feature. Jim said the tuna would probably be over two hundred pounds once we got it weighed at the dock. Although we had not found a shark, I was plenty excited to have caught such a large tuna on my very first attempt at live bait trolling in Hawaiian waters. Jim offered to radio ahead and the charter agency called Nancy so she could meet us at the dock. Once the *Lei Aloha* tied up at the Kailua Bay weigh station, our tuna tipped the scales at two hundred and one pounds. It was almost like an unbelievable dream. Fortunately I still have the picture that was taken to always remind me of a great day on the water.

Still wanting to have a chance to catch a Pacific blue marlin before leaving for home, I told Jim I wanted to charter him for one more day. We worked out a full-day charter for two days later. I figured I might never be in Hawaii again, so why not try to have the very best fishing experience possible. Hindsight proved this was a good decision. Using the very same trolling techniques with live skipjack tuna as baits, I was able to hook and land not one, but two, Pacific blue marlin. Each of these fish lit up with spectacular iridescent colors during and after the fight, and both tried to throw the hook with multiple magnificent jumps. One of the marlin weighed in at one hundred fifty-seven pounds while the second marlin tipped the scales at two hundred fourteen pounds! They were not huge by Pacific marlin standards, but they fought hard and jumped spectacularly, and I was thrilled to have caught not one but two marlin in the same day! When we got back to the dock, Jim explained to me that what I had experienced had not been a typical day of marlin fishing. Where I had assumed that two marlin had been an average day of fishing in paradise, he quickly assured me that some of his clients had spent day after day after day and enormous amounts of money in search of that first elusive blue marlin. When I heard that, I felt even better about the day we had just had, and I thanked Jim and Randy for an outstanding two days of fishing in Hawaii.

The day after the marlin charter, as we were starting to pack to leave Hawaii, the phone in our hotel room rang and it was Jim Hunter. He wanted to know if he could stop by before we left but wouldn't say why.

"Sure, come on over. You can join us for breakfast."

When he met Nancy and me at breakfast, he proceeded to say how much he had enjoyed having me as a charter, particularly since I knew what to do once hooked up to a large game fish. I thanked him for the expression of confidence, and then he handed me a present which he asked me to unwrap. As I removed the wrapping paper, a beautiful miniature replica mount of a hammerhead shark became visible. The fish was mounted on an oval wooden plaque with the word *mano* spelled out in shark's teeth beneath the shark.

Nancy asked Jim what *mano* meant. I already knew it meant hand in Spanish but had no idea why it would be on this mount. Jim explained that *mano* was the Hawaiian word for shark. He said that since I had tried so hard to catch a shark in Hawaii, he wanted us to have the mount as a remembrance of him, Randy, and the charter. Nancy and I both enjoyed his company through breakfast and thanked him again before he left to prepare for another charter. Today that shark mount still holds a special place on our family room wall. I guess in a manner of speaking, I finally did get a shark in Hawaii!

Captain's Tip: When in Rome, do as the Romans. Always defer to the local pros and trust their expertise and game plan. Local captains fish in their area day in and day out, usually with excellent success.

Much of fishing knowledge is region specific. The local way is usually the path to greatest results!

Captain's Log: Randy Parker, the mate on my charters, is the son of George "Marlin" Parker, a pioneer in the evolution of Hawaiian big game fishing. For his groundbreaking efforts, George Parker was recently enshrined in the I.G.F.A. Hall of Fame in Dania Beach, Florida, near Fort Lauderdale. Randy, now a licensed captain, runs his own charter boat, *Bad Company*, in Hawaii.

Mike Halperin on left, Captain Jim Hunter, and Mate Randy Parker on right with author's 201-pound yellowfin tuna in Kailua-Kona, Hawaii.

Mike Halperin on left, Captain Jim Hunter standing, Mate Randy Parker kneeling with author's Pacific blue marlin of 157- and 214-pounds in Kailua-Kona, Hawaii.

6

A Thanksgiving to Remember

IT WAS ONE OF those crisp, clear, sunny November days that normally occurs after a strong high front moves through an area. Early that morning, Craig Paige and I were off again on another fishing adventure. We had fueled my nineteen-foot Bayliner, loaded up with ice, bait, rods and reels, lures, and other tackle, and headed east into the Atlantic Ocean toward Chesapeake Light Tower. It was Thanksgiving weekend in the early 1970s, and we were hoping to intercept the fall migration of bluefish as they schooled to leave Chesapeake Bay and head south. We were also anticipating finding some of the bluefish we knew would be traveling down the East Coast from their traditional haunts in New England.

About twenty minutes after leaving Cape Henry in our wake, Chesapeake Light Tower came into view. This nautical landmark marks the turning point at the beginning of the ocean entrance to Chesapeake Bay for all manner of military and commercial ships. This site was first established in 1930 as an active lightship station. The lightship *Chesapeake*, now in Baltimore's Inner Harbor, guided mariners in and out of the Chesapeake Bay from 1933 to 1965. Excluding WWII, the *Chesapeake* remained on station through this period. In 1965, the lightship was replaced by a manned light tower that is 120 feet high. The light was automated in 1980 and the structure currently serves as a site for scientific experiments by NOAA. The tower's original boat landing was destroyed by Hurricane Isabel, and the tower can now only be reached by helicopter.

As we sped toward this tower, four small white specs slowly grew larger and became visible as the only boats present. We discussed the small number of boats and decided we would have little difficulty finding fishing room around the structure. Most other people were probably home eating their Thanksgiving turkey and watching football. What a shame. More bluefish for us!

Craig rummaged in our gear and promptly chose two premier swimming bluefish plugs. He then rigged these two red and white Cisco Kid lures on medium weight trolling rods. These lures had become Chesapeake Bay classics in the sixties and seventies, definitely not from appearance but from results in putting fish onboard. Since purchasing a boat and becoming a bay fishing fanatic, I had gone from being highly skeptical to a true believer in the Cisco Kid. It had a bright red painted head, two conspicuous black eyes, and a light-reflecting plastic prismatic body with a life-like fish scale pattern under a hard plastic shell. Three sets of dangling treble hooks completed the lure. For safety and ease of unhooking we were known to replace the three treble hooks with single hooks or even a lone hook hanging from the back of the lure. Most importantly, each Cisco Kid lure had a wide metal lip that could be bent infinitely to adjust its angle of dive and the subsequent depth at which the lure would run. With immediate depths around the tower running from forty to sixty feet, we decided to run one lure on an in-line sinker on the first rod. The other lure was set to run off a three-way swivel with a three-foot drop to a sinker that allowed the lure to work just off the bottom.

WITH THIS GEAR STREAMED OUT, we began to slowly troll around the light tower and its surrounding mini plateau where the bottom comes up to a depth of forty feet in the adjacent sixty-five-foot water. It was a beautiful, sunny flat calm day as we proceeded to troll in slow, elliptical circles around the tower. Sometimes we would do a lazy S curve or slow down and speed up to impart more action to the lures. Nothing happened. No bluefish. No hits. We had to settle for the peace and tranquility of the outdoors and the glistening Atlantic waters.

After a couple of hours of working hard we were ready to quit. In a last attempt to catch something, we decided to work our lures closer to the tower. As we passed the southeast corner of the tower mid-afternoon in about forty feet of water, the rod just off the bottom began to jerk as if it had hooked a fish. However, it did not create the drag-pulling reel-screaming event we had been hoping to hear. Just one or two twelve or thirteen pound blue fish would have made our whole trip worthwhile. As Craig reeled in the line and the lure, the fish finally started to become visible a few feet below the surface. We both stared as we focused four disbelieving eyes on about a two and half pound flounder that was firmly attached to the Cisco Kid lure. Even though this was not the game plan for the day, it elicited excited cries of joy at having finally caught a fish, *any* fish!

After we both tried to determine if the fish had bitten the lure or been foul hooked off the bottom, we realized it did not really matter. We both knew that if there was one flounder down there, there were likely to be a whole lot more. Flounder are territorial and particularly prone to schooling and feeding as they work through their fall feeding and migration patterns. As quickly as we could, we pulled in the trolling rigs. We then hurriedly rigged our terminal gear with two high-low bottom rigs, baited the hooks with squid strips, and began to drift back through the area where we had just caught the flounder.

As soon as our rigs hit bottom, they were forcefully bitten with characteristic flounder taps, and we began making steady hookups. The fishing was so good that we eventually started leaving the rigs in the water with the first fish on in hopes of hooking a second flounder on the same drop. In many cases we did just that. Quickly we also discovered that the fish were packed in a relatively small area just off the southeast corner of the tower. Once the boat drifted past the end of the school, the bites stopped as if someone had turned off a switch. After two drifts, we knew just what area the flounder were in and kept repeating tight short drifts in this pattern. The only problem was deciding whether or not to cut up one or two of the flounder for more bait as our squid supply started to dwindle. Tough problem to have! Even though we were starting to get tired from cranking up so many fish, this bait and hook flounder rodeo went on through most of the mid-afternoon with loads of flounder coming aboard. After a while we even stopped using the net and just swung the flounder into the boat if they looked securely hooked. We knew there were plenty more out there if one should happen to fall back in the water on the way into the boat. This was definitely the best day either one of us had ever enjoyed flounder fishing. We both regretted that Craig's father had declined our offer to come with us. Boy, would he be surprised when we got home!

With the late November sunset coming around 5 P.M., we decided to head in when the sun started to dip since we had a long run back to Lynnhaven Inlet in Virginia Beach. By heading in at 3:30, we hoped to be off the big water before dark. When we arrived at the dock late with little or no daylight left, we opted to leave the cleaning of the boat for the next day and drove together to Craig's house to divide our catch. By then it was dark, and the easiest way to split the fish was to use his driveway and outdoor floodlights. We proceeded to dump all the flounder in Craig's driveway. I knew we had done well, but until Craig counted a total of seventy-five fish I had no idea how well. Almost all of the fish were between three and five pounds with a lot of four and five pounders mixed in! I spent most of the next day scaling, filleting, and freezing fish. Needless to say, we both enjoyed flounder through that winter, and I even gave some away so that all the fish would be eaten.

This had been a learning experience from the ocean. We had found flounder in a way and in an area at a time where we would not have expected them. Truly a Thanksgiving I shall always remember!

Captain's Tip: Note that this excursion took place in the early 1970s before Virginia had bag or size limits on many fish. Being young, naïve, and foolish, we were not wise enough to impose our own bag limits for the resource as we should have. I would encourage all anglers to keep only what they can reasonably eat and use. Tag and/or release the rest. Today this is not a problem as most saltwater species are strictly regulated. For those that aren't, we all need to use common sense.

Two typical Chesapeake Bay flounder

7

A Monumental Catch by Non-Design

AUGUST 14th, 1982, IS a day I shall always remember as if it were yesterday, and yet it is already more than twenty-five years ago. It was an era that was the heyday of "jaws" mania for many fishermen along the coastal United States. This was in large part due to the release of the movie *Jaws* by author Eric Benchley. Sharks had suddenly become the working man's marlin and were on everyone's desired catch list. Hundreds of anglers were determined to catch a BIG shark!

Personally, this era could not have come at a better time for me. I was thirty-five years old, had become a fairly accomplished angler through study and experience, and owned our second boat, a twenty-four foot walk-a-round that was ocean/offshore capable on many good-weather summer days. As a former athlete and current physical education teacher, I was well conditioned for physical strength and stamina—two of the attributes most needed to defeat and capture large pelagic game fish. Having learned some of the finer points of shark fishing from one of my former students, Craig Paige, I was now eager to charge offshore with friends in search of large sharks.

Lamentably, my almost brand-new beautiful boat was yet again out of commission. Subsequently I would find out that the screen on a fuel tank line was picking up sediment from the gas tank and blocking the flow of fuel to the engine any time the seas started to get rough. As the dealer had yet to find and correct this continued problem, I was without a boat and feeling miserable at the very height of the summer shark season.

One day I was walking down the dock and stopped to talk to one of the fellow shark experts at my marina, Jimmy Stokes. Jimmy had a fantastic twenty-six foot Sea Ray Amberjack named *Second Love* that was perfectly suited for shark trips in the Atlantic. He clearly knew what he was doing and had been consistently hooking up with three hundred to five hundred-pound tiger sharks on an almost regular basis. After talking with me, I think he felt sorry for me because my boat had been awaiting repair for so long. Somehow when the conversation got around to shark fishing, he decided to invite me to go with him on his next trip. Needless to say, I was beyond ecstatic. Jimmy usually fished for sharks with two other very knowledgeable anglers. Keith Casiano was an accomplished fisherman whose father was a commercial fisherman, and David Tugwell was a fellow member of the fishing club I belonged to named the Virginia Beach Sharkers. I thought to myself that the four of us would make an unbeatable team!

As usual, our off-shore trip began well before sunrise in August to take advantage of the calm early morning seas. On the trip out we talked about our jobs and mutual love of fishing. I asked how successful they had been in locating large sharks that season.

"Well, when the weather permits, the three of us fish almost every weekend," Keith told me.

"Yeah, and we usually come back with at least one shark over five hundred pounds," David chimed in. "Jimmy likes to quit and head in after we have one good fish, or we'd probably come in with two or three close to that size."

"It sounds as if we're going to have a fantastic trip."

From the helm, Jimmy finally joined the conversation.

"Mike, I'd be pretty surprised if we don't pick up at least one large citation shark where we're headed today."

That morning there was a light one-foot wave chop on top of gentle ocean swells. Jimmy put us on a course southeast from Cape Henry and just headed further and further out. The farther we went, the calmer it seemed to get. When we were about thirty-five miles from Cape Henry, the ocean surface was flat, but this also meant there was no breeze to provide any relief from the heat. I had a pretty good idea where he was going in general, but he never really would let me see his honey hole on the chart or the pre-programmed loran numbers with which he was navigating. Months later, Jimmy eventually did share with me exactly where we had fished. The area where we had been fishing was on the edge of a U-shaped sea mount, appropriately named "The Horseshoe." I must have earned his confidence by then.

We finally got to the grounds after about a two-hour run and anchored. I remember being careful that day to bring only one fishing rod and to allow them to get their lines in first. As the proverbial "guest," I did not want to upset their routine or get in the way as this threesome always fished together on a regular basis. We had more fresh bait than we knew what to do with since they had caught some Boston mackerel during the spring run and frozen a large batch that was now defrosting.

I decided to fish one of my twisted piano wire rigs with two 14/0 hooks and my usual nylon-coated cable leader with the one custom rod and matching 12/0 reel spooled with 130-pound Dacron line. Within a short time after putting a whole one-pound mackerel on as bait, I got a strong and steady run off. Once I set the hook hard the first of three times, I knew I had a good fish. It was going to be a long morning. Keith and David knew the drill and were great! They quickly cleared all the other rigs, racked up the rods, and stowed the baits out of the way. After I had been fighting the fish a while, I re-member Jimmy releasing an anchor marker flag and float that was al-ready attached to a cleat and placed overboard prior to fishing. This was done by design to allow us to leave the anchor and pursue the fish with the boat, thus preventing a large shark from stripping all the line from the reel. It also allowed us to go back and retrieve the anchor once the fish was captured. Sometimes this could be a few miles away and more than an hour or two later. By punching in the loran num-bers when the float was released, the anchor was much easier to find, even if the flag was hard to see in rough seas.

JIMMY STAYED AT THE CONTROLS and proceeded to deftly spin the *Second Love*, using the twin engines to constantly keep the fish positioned directly off the stern. The fish kept trying to circle the boat, but Jimmy kept using the throttles to beat him at his game. With Jimmy's expert boat handling and our well-coordinated team-work, I was convinced I could beat this fish as long as I paced myself and didn't try to apply too much drag.

It was fast becoming a battle between my stamina and the shark's dogged determination to free himself through his seemingly unend-ing energy. I was beginning to sweat profusely in the hot August sun and was worried about muscle cramps setting in. David and Keith would periodically hand me a cold drink while I would simply hold the rod with one hand. After about an hour, the fish was slowly start-ing to be pulled toward the boat inch by sweaty inch. At times it would make a powerful run and I would have to work yet again to re-gain all the lost line. At the end of twenty more minutes, the shark fi-nally was visible on the surface, but he still had considerable fight left in him. At first glance, his dorsal fin protruded high above the surface and he looked huge, but his size was hard to judge at a distance. If the hooks continued to hold, and I could work him to the side of the boat, we would probably have a much better idea of his true size and weight.

THAT THIS FISH HAD NOT GIVEN UP yet was clearly evidenced by the need for continued multiple attempts at line retrieval coupled with many leader releases before the crew could ultimately gain control of the leader. When the fish was finally brought near the boat, the importance of safety and teamwork was brought home to me by this outstanding crew. They worked together on securing a tail rope.

"Now, David, I slid the tail rope in position, and I'm going to need all the help you can give me once I jerk it tight and lift his tail."

"No problem, Keith, I've already put on my gloves. Just tell me when."

Jimmy remained at the helm, keeping a now clearly identified dusky shark calm by pulling him and aerating his gills using the boat's slight forward headway.

At the appropriate moment, Keith and David snatched the shark's tail with a tail rope and immediately tied it off to a stern cleat until the fish settled down.

"We've got him now," Keith yelled. "Give me two more tail ropes."

Next came more lines for full control, culminating with all four of us working together to physically pull the fish in to the boat. Using a come-a-long and a transom roller, we worked together to slowly pull the fish tail first over the transom and into the boat for the ride home. Jimmy was a real craftsman when it came to machine-shop work and had made a clever roller system that was sturdily mounted to the transom of the *Second Love*. With enough manpower, there were few—if any—fish he could not load into his boat. Once cranked in, the shark's head and upper body lay on the motor box and transom while the rest of him landed with a thud on the cockpit deck. The shark's length extended from the steering station all the way to the boat's transom. Everyone else had now broken a sweat. Catching this shark was hard enough; getting him physically into the boat had turned into an equally daunting task. Judging from the shark's enormous length and girth, we estimated he weighed at least five hundred pounds.

I was elated and exhausted. At that point a little food, a lot of water, and some adrenalin kept me going. As was Jimmy's custom, once a respectable shark had been boated, fishing would stop and he would head to shore knowing it would be a long trip with either a fish in tow or, as in our case, a lot of additional weight in the boat. On the way in to the marina, I decided to wire the shark's jaws shut. This would help to maintain its weight by preventing loss of fluids prior to weigh in. Based on my familiarity with other dusky sharks I had caught, I realized that this was a *very* large catch.

When we arrived at our homeport at Lynnhaven Waterway Marina, a fork lift had to be used with a tail rope to lift the enormous fish out of Jimmy's boat. As the lift picked it up over the bulkhead, it seemed to get bigger and bigger until its whole length became visible in a vertical plain. Once the fish was weighed, Jimmy grabbed some white chalk and wrote the digits 673 on the side of the fish. That was when it hit me that I had just broken the Virginia state record for dusky sharks!

While one part of me was very excited, I felt bad that I had kept Jimmy and his friends from fishing any more on that day. However, they were all great about it and could not have been happier to have had a part in it. In fact, we all went out that night to celebrate the day's accomplishment. Many thanks to Jimmy Stokes, Keith Casiano, and David Tugwell for sharing this fishing experience with me and allowing me into their inner circle on that day. I will always be grateful for the memories!

Captain's Tip: Always proceed cautiously when working a large fish. A marked change in the fish's behavior will let you know when it is safe to leader and capture it. Never attempt to lift a shark's tail out of the water until you have firmly attached a tail rope to the fish and are about to secure the line to the boat.

Captain's Note: This was a particularly heartwarming state record to get as I had once previously taken over the state lead for dusky shark during a Virginia Beach Sharker's Tournament only to be bested shortly thereafter by one of my fellow Sharkers.

Postscript: A 2006 winter visit to the IGFA Hall of Fame near Fort Lauderdale revealed that the dusky shark I caught in 1982 continues to be the second largest dusky shark on record anywhere. The only heavier recorded dusky shark is Warren Girle's world record at 764 pounds, also caught in 1982 at Longboat Key, Florida.

673-pound Virginia state record dusky shark and second-largest dusky shark on record.

8

Murphy's Law Hard at Work

TO PARAPHRASE A GREAT line from Charles Dickens, it was the best of days and it was the worst of days. It was an oppressively hot, sticky July morning in Virginia. The weather service gave the usual summer forecast. "Hot, hazy, and humid with a forty percent chance of thunderstorms."

After hearing this forecast, and since the winds were light southwest, Sam Doyle and I headed offshore into the Atlantic Ocean for a day of shark fishing. Sam, who shared my love of fishing and whose daughter I had coached in softball, was excited about having a chance to catch a big shark. We would be doing battle in my twenty-four foot Sea Ray walk-a-round cuddy cabin.

After leaving Lynnhaven Inlet, we literally sprinted at thirty miles an hour across the nearly calm Atlantic Ocean. Slowly the boat rose up and over the long ocean swells with only an occasional thump for a few small errant waves. It was a delightful roller coaster ride at sea, particularly for me as the helmsman standing with flexed knees to maintain balance as I sensed the motion of the boat over the swells. There is no better way for a fisherman to commune with nature than to feel water fleeting away under a boat and to breathe the fresh smell of salt air. The magnificent sunrise in the eastern sky on this particular day added to the grandeur of the experience.

My intended destination on a heading of 106 degrees east by southeast was Chesapeake Light Tower. The tower is immediately adjacent to one of the largest and most productive of the numerous Tidewater artificial reefs scattered in the Chesapeake Bay and the ocean. The Tower Reef teems with all types of seasonal fish. However, on this day when we reached Chesapeake Light Tower, I turned the

51

bow due southeast and ran a compass course for about seven nautical miles to an area of lumpy bottom. I was quite certain this area
would yield a large shark.

Having left the dock before daylight, we were now in a position
to be fishing by 7:30 A.M. with a chum slick and lines in the water. My
intent with such an early start had been threefold: first, to beat some
of the worst heat of the day and, I hoped, the afternoon thunderstorms; second, to take advantage of the usually flat summer morning seas for a quick run to the grounds; and third, to be sure to allow
plenty of time to fight, capture, and tow a large shark (if necessary)
before the waves increased with the afternoon breeze.

WHEN WE ARRIVED at the chosen fishing area, I assessed the current and wind to plan our pending drift. I asked Sam to assist me in
preparing chum and baits. On a hot day, this could be the least desirable part of our fishing preparation.

"Sam, this is going to be the most fun you are going to have
today," I said with a smile.

Sam wasn't quite sure what I meant as he looked at me quizzi-
cally. I handed him one of the four bricks of chum I had stored in my
rugged time-worn ninety-six-quart Igloo cooler. The bricks were the
result of chopping a fifty-pound bag of frozen ground fish into four
equivalent pieces that morning. These bags were commonly referred
to as "mink food" at the processing plant where I purchased them.
If only the women who eventually bought mink stoles knew what
those mink had been eating! As I passed the brick of chum to Sam, I
held on to the remaining wrapping paper that surrounded it and the
brick fell neatly into the five-gallon chum bucket that Sam was holding. I always initially left the paper on the bricks to keep them from
defrosting too quickly in the summer heat.

By now Sam could smell the strong odor of the slowly defrosting chum and had figured out what I had meant by "most fun." As
I started to rig our shark baits, Sam tied the bucket top closed, looped
it over a stern cleat, and slipped it over the side where it would rock
in the water with the boat's motion.

"Is unwrapping chum just a rite of initiation, or is that why you
always bring a guest with you?" Sam quipped. We now had an instant chum slick. Bits of ground fish began to slowly disperse through
the myriad of half-inch holes drilled in the bucket's sides and bottom. As was my habit, I shook the bucket three times to *jump start*
the slick and for good luck.

Within an hour we had our first finned customer peeling off line.
I insisted that Sam fight the first shark that showed up because he

was my guest. He did an admirable job using a 6/0 Penn Senator rod and reel outfit that was spooled with 50-pound test Dacron line. After a lengthy struggle, Sam had worked a good-sized brown shark next to the boat. Since I hoped to hook up with some considerably larger sharks as the day progressed, the fish was quickly tagged and released. Over the next few hours we alternately hooked, tagged, and released several more sandbar (brown) sharks over one hundred pounds.

By 9:30 A.M., the sky far to the west was turning black and the weather was starting to look very foreboding. It was time to plan for our return to port.

"Sam, let's fish thirty more minutes or catch one more shark, whichever comes first, and then we'll head for the inlet." Since Sam was looking at the same darkening sky, I got no argument from him.

"Okay, we've already caught several nice sharks, and I don't want to get caught out here in any thunderstorms."

Right after this conversation, the 6/0 reel went off again.

"You take it, Sam."

Sam grabbed the rod from the gunwale and struck the fish to set the hook. The fish was apparently stronger than our prior sharks and proved it by making several strong runs away from the boat. Sam, however, was not going to be deterred. I also knew he wanted to get this fish in so we could stow our gear and head for the dock as soon as possible. After a short but intense battle of twenty minutes, Sam had the fish headed toward the surface and close to the boat. As soon as the fish surfaced, I began to get excited. The fish Sam had subdued was a shark of about one hundred and thirty pounds.

"Sam, we're not tagging this one. We're going to bring it in because it is such an unlikely catch."

The fish was now close enough that Sam could see I was beginning to leader a hammerhead shark to the boat. As hammerhead sharks were an unusual catch for Virginia waters, I told Sam that catching such a fish was truly unique. I quickly tail roped the hammerhead, and then the two of us strained to pull it over the roller bar that was mounted on my stern transom. This heavy duty trailer roller had been carefully attached to the transom specifically to serve as an aide for boating large sharks and other fish. Once we wrestled the shark over the transom and onto the cockpit deck, we tied it off securely as we did not want to risk feeling the pain of its razor sharp teeth. Tying off the shark would also prevent damage to the cockpit during the ride home.

I walked to the steering station and turned the key in the ignition. I got a grinding sound, but the engine refused to start. I waited a few moments in case it was flooded and then tried to start it again. Again nothing happened but the grinding of the starter motor.

"Sam, the dealer was supposed to have fixed this for me since my last trip when it also failed to start."

I looked at Sam's face as I spoke and saw a growing look of concern. A quick glance at the sky showed us that it was darkening further, and also the wind was intensifying.

"Let's do this. You drop the anchor and I'll call the Coast Guard for towing assistance."

In the 1980s the U. S. Coast Guard would still assist in a non-emergency situation. Since then, massive federal budget cuts have forced the Coast Guard to limit its responses to serious emergencies such as sinking or fire. I grabbed the microphone of my VHF radio which was already set on channel 16, and waited for a break in transmissions.

"Coast Guard Little Creek, Coast Guard Little Creek, this is the vessel *Drifter,* over." Almost immediately a response boomed back. "*Drifter,* this is Group Hampton Roads Little Creek, over."

I shared the nature of our problem and answered all the usual Coast Guard queries about size and color of my vessel and number of people on board. Then came the obligatory order to put on life jackets. I also gave my exact position with Loran coordinates and was instructed to stand by on the radio. Several minutes later the Coast Guard came back on the radio confirming that they had dispatched a forty-one foot cutter to come and get us. Estimated time of arrival was one hour.

SAM AND I SAT and waited as we watched the seas continue to build from the now brisk wind. We were not in any danger but were starting to get very uncomfortable from the building seas. We settled in to wait, knowing a long afternoon was still ahead of us. All we could do was sit on the twin helm seats and stare at the business end of Sam's hammerhead, wondering how long help would take to get to us. After about fifty minutes, a large white boat with an orange stripe on the bow came into view over the horizon. Help was now imminent, or so we thought.

When the Coast Guard cutter approached our boat, we were asked to secure a towing bridle to the bow, which situated us about seventy feet behind the cutter. Their coxswain quickly took up the strain on the line, and we were told by radio to just steer as they began to tow us the seventeen miles to Cape Henry. The ride to the Cape that the Coast Guard gave us could best be termed a "Nantucket sleigh ride." This term owes its origin to the ride the old whalers would get in their dories after harpooning a whale. Our tow quickly turned in to a wild bone-jarring ride. I radioed my concern to the Coast Guard cutter that maybe they could slow down a bit so we would not take such a physical beating on the waves. They seemed to be relentless in their speed without much regard for the occupants of the craft they were towing. Sam and I thought perhaps they had another emergency to go to, or maybe they felt they needed to "punish" mariners or fishermen who managed to cause them work by breaking down offshore. Although the building storm missed us, we still endured a very rough return trip.

After taking a pounding for almost an hour, the Cape Henry Lighthouse was a very welcome sight indeed. Once the cutter approached the Lesner Bridge at the entrance to Lynnhaven Inlet, the Coast Guard crew slowed to idle speed. After passing under the bridge, they shortened and retied the tow line. Using three huge round fenders they "rafted" or tied us side to side on their port side, saying they would carry us this way for the rest of the trip to our marina. In this coupled fashion, they motored us up the creek toward my homeport at Lynnhaven Dry Storage Marina on Long Creek.

All was going well until the Coast Guard coxswain began to make his turn to port to enter the narrow waterway leading to the dry storage docks. At that moment, Murphy's Law struck. A very strong outgoing tide started to push the Coast Guard boat and my boat simultaneously toward a row of boats that were moored on our port side. Those boats were in slips bordering the creek. The seaman running the Coast Guard boat quickly lost control of his craft in the swift current. As the tide continued to sweep him downstream, it was becoming apparent that my boat was about to become the "ham" in a very undesirable "ham sandwich" between a steel-hulled forty-one foot Coast Guard cutter and the pointed bows of four or five docked boats.

Sam wanted to help. "Let me try to fend off on our port side." he yelled.

It would be almost impossible for him to do that.

"Don't do it. The force of impact will be too great, and I don't want you to get hurt!" In spite of my warning, Sam attempted to do the best he could. Nevertheless, we were doomed to be raked across the sharp bows of several boats with the force of the heavy Coast Guard vessel pressing us against them. The coxswain continued to struggle to try to regain control of his vessel. No such luck. *Crack, crunch, crunch, crack...* the agonizing sounds went as our port gunwale was broken and torn up by consecutive bow to gunwale impacts. My disbelief at what was happening quickly turned to anger as I realized that we were totally powerless to stop it. Ironically and frighteningly, it was the Coast Guard which was supposed to be *rescuing* us rather than creating mayhem and extensive damage.

As the coxswain remained unable to regain control of his boat in the swift current, Sam and I quickly untied from their boat to minimize the damage. Once we were free, we "walked" our boat by hand to one of the piers where we finally tied off. The two of us then examined the damage and waited for the impending boarding and inspection I knew was coming. My bow rail was twisted like a pretzel and no longer fully attached to the deck. There were large scrapes and deep gouges in the fiberglass on the port side. Even though the cutter's crew had torn up my boat, I knew we would be forced to endure a safety inspection since they had responded to an emergency assistance call. That, too, quickly turned into another unexpected ordeal.

When the Coast Guardsman they dispatched on the dock to inspect us saw Sam's large hammerhead shark lying in the bottom of the boat, he refused to come aboard to do the inspection. I tried to dispel his fears. "That shark has been stone cold dead for over two hours."

"I don't care. I'm not going anywhere near him or your boat, Captain!"

That was the only statement I was to get from the man in Coast Guard blue with the clipboard before he rapidly departed.

About ten minutes later, following a quickly held conference on board the Coast Guard cutter, another member of the cutter's crew finally ambled down the dock to do the inspection. We passed with flying colors as I knew we would. Of course he wanted to see all the usual safety items: flares, life jackets, throwable cushion, registration, etc. Once that formality was concluded, I asked that their very embarrassed coxswain talk with me regarding the damage he had caused to my boat.

I made a point of thanking him and his crew for towing us to port, but then made it very clear that the Coast Guard should be responsible for paying for the damage they had caused. I also vowed to myself that my next boat would have twin engines. I *never* again wanted to be left in a similar helpless situation. As it later turned out, my next two boats were in fact twin-engine sportfishing boats.

Now that the Coast Guard had finished its inspection, we could turn our attention to weighing Sam's shark. Sam and I watched expectantly as the fish was suspended from an official scale and registered a very respectable 139 pounds. I congratulated Sam again since this weight now officially qualified him for a Virginia State Fishing Tournament citation for his hammerhead shark. Not only did Sam Doyle get a colorful citation plaque, but he had a story to tell that I know he will never forget. With a little luck, remembering the success we had during the fishing part of our trip, maybe Sam would even want to fish with me again.

Captain's Tip: It is best to avoid breaking down offshore by keeping your boat well maintained. Keep radio contact with other boats near you who may provide assistance if needed. Better yet, if you can afford it, buy a boat with twin engines!

9

More Than One Way To Skin A Cat

IT ALL STARTED WITH my generous offer to donate an all-expense paid shark fishing trip as a goodwill and public relations gesture for my shark fishing club, the Virginia Beach Sharkers. I would provide the boat and serve as captain, and a fellow club member and experienced shark fisherman would tag along and serve as an expert "mate." The Sharkers would reimburse me for all of my fuel expenses. What could be simpler or more fun, I thought.

The club always manned a public service booth in the fishing section of the annual Mid-Atlantic Boat Show in Virginia Beach every February. The eventual "trip" winners were the result of a club raffle at the boat show. Following the boat show, I learned that a married couple would be my guests for a Saturday of sport fishing aboard *Ocean Venture*, my thirty-two-foot Wellcraft sportfisherman. Brad Harvey, accomplished fisherman and well over six feet tall and two hundred pounds, was to be the mate. I was really pleased to have Brad as he not only knew exactly what to do as a shark fisherman but was strong enough to hold on to any leader regardless of what type of shark it might be attached to! In a few quick follow up phone calls I had our fishing date confirmed with all participants. While unknown to me initially, it soon became readily apparent that Murphy's Law was to be hard at work on this angling adventure.

About 9:30 the night before the trip, Brad Harvey called to inform me that he HAD to go to work at his day job the next day.

"Brad, what do you mean you HAVE to work?"

Brad could probably detect the anger and disappointment in my voice as he tried to explain that he had been called in by our local electric company and that it was imperative that he report to deal with a major power problem. I certainly understood the gravity of his need to report to work. However, by the time I hung up I knew what a difficult time I could be facing the next day without an experienced mate to assist me. At literally the eleventh hour, I made a few quick phone calls to club members to ask if they would be able to fill in for Brad. In each case, the answer was a resounding no, primarily because of the extreme short notice. It was late, so I decided to turn in and get some rest before the next day's fishing.

In spite of the events of the night before, Saturday dawned under a bright, hot sun with barely a breath of wind. At least the weather was going to cooperate! After a quick shower and breakfast, I drove down to *Ocean Venture* to do some pre-fishing prep work for the club winners' charter. People who have fished with me know I have an almost compulsive need for everything to be totally prepared and organized prior to leaving the dock and certainly before guests or fishing buddies arrive. When shark fishing, this pays double dividends in the area of safety. Gaffs, tail ropes, leaders, hook rigs, baits, chum, and rods and reels all need to be arranged and stowed for safety and ease of access.

Promptly at 7:00 A.M., the raffle winning couple came strolling down the dock. I stepped off the boat to greet them, helped them stow their food and gear, and then gave them a quick orientation to all the safety gear on the boat ranging from life preservers to the EPIRB and life raft. I must say that I felt some "unofficial" added pressure when I learned that my male guest was the direct boss of one of our club members. In addition to the normal desire to have a successful day on the water, it would be very bad public relations to get skunked.

In a few moments *Ocean Venture* was idling out of Lynnhaven Inlet, and once we passed under the Lesner Bridge I pushed the twin throttles forward and the twin Mercruiser engines settled in at a twenty-eight mile-per-hour cruise speed. As we reached Cape Henry, I steered southeast heading toward an area I anticipated would hold sharks. Forty minutes later I eased back off the throttles and the boat came off plane. We were approximately twenty miles off Virginia Beach. It was a great day to be alive and an even better day to be fishing. As my charter guests were new to ocean sport fishing, they were instructed to just relax while I started chumming and began to rig baits and leaders.

Since I was fishing without a mate and we were in sixty-foot-deep water, I decided I would only put out two shark fishing rigs, knowing it would be hectic enough to just clear the one extra rig once we hooked up with a fish. I also decided to drift rather than anchor, as this would permit us to fight any fish much more quickly and successfully. Anchors can be a time-delaying pain to deal with when a large fish is hooked up.

One rig was on a 6/0 Penn reel I had won in one of our shark fishing tournaments, and it was set out on a float on the surface with a bright yellow balloon for visibility. The other was on a 9/0 Penn mounted on a custom-made rod with bright brown and white wraps, and it was on the bottom almost directly under the boat with a large tuna head. The float bait dangled a small, tempting strip of skipjack tuna belly. Both baits were impaled with double hook rigs with hand twisted number 19 wire since I wanted to maximize the chance of hooking up. Within a few minutes of the baits and chum going into the water, seagulls began to dive and soar in and out of the growing chum slick. As the birds picked out bits of fish they provided us with morning entertainment.

After about an hour, the clicker on the float rig began to go off, but not with the authority of any type of real solid pick-up. I quickly grabbed the rod, set the hook, and proceeded to watch a fair-sized dolphin light up the ocean with its blue and green iridescent colors as it raced rapidly back and forth across the sea surface trying to regain its freedom. I handed the rod to my female fishing guest and coached her to keep a tight line while reeling in the fish. Even with an inexperienced angler on the other end of the line, the dolphin had no chance of getting free as he was slowly cranked in on the 6/0 reel. While complimenting and congratulating her on the good job she was doing, I silently hoped that a bigger fish would wander into our baits. A few short minutes went by, and I deftly gaffed the dolphin while simultaneously dropping him into our chum and bait cooler and slamming the lid shut. My guests sat on the cooler lid to keep the dolphin from escaping into the cockpit, and I told them they could not move until all noise coming from the cooler had stopped!

By now I was silently talking to myself. *Are there **ANY** sharks **ANY PLACE** near here?*

An hour and a half after our lone dolphin and three hours after starting our chum slick and seeing no other fish of any kind, I announced a change of game plan, "I think we should move to a different area to continue our fishing." As we had not seen a shark, my guests were more than agreeable.

THEY HELPED ME pull in the baits, stow them on ice, and pull up the chum bucket. We headed northeast at a brisk cruise speed, and the air blowing in our faces provided some relief from the sweltering August heat. About fifteen minutes later I felt we had reached some good lumpy bottom with underwater ridges and travel pathways for migrating sharks, so I slowed the boat to a stop. We were all sorry to lose the temporary rush of cooling air that had refreshed us as we sped along to our new location.

Once more the baits were carefully placed in the water. The chum bucket was reloaded with a new brick of somewhat frozen ground mink food (fish meal) and lowered back into the ocean to again work its magic from a stern cleat. It was time to get under the canvas top away from the baking sun.

The three of us had been relaxing for fifteen minutes and were close to dozing off from the heat when the clicker on the 9/0 reel began to signal Dacron line peeling off steadily. I had my angler put on a pair of thick leather gloves to protect his hands for the coming battle. He was already wearing a gimbal belt, so I told him to stand up while I slipped my custom made shoulder harness on him and clipped it into two attachment lugs on the top of the reel. Thanks to my wife, Nancy, I have one of the best fighting harnesses ever made. At my request she had taken the Dacron fabric from my U.S. Navy duffel bag and sewn it into one of the lightest, strongest, and best-looking harnesses.

Then, as I had instructed him earlier, he placed the rod butt in the gimbal of his fighting belt, lowered the rod tip directly toward the disappearing line, and prepared to place both gloved thumbs as tightly as he could against the line on the reel. When I yelled "Now!" that would be the signal for him to move the lever that would throw the reel in gear, lock his thumbs down against the line, and strike as hard as he could with the rod.

"*Now!*"

At my command he struck the fish by pulling back hard on the rod. Then I yelled to him a second time. "*Strike him again!*"

As he finished lowering the rod tip, the line instantly came tight. He winced and pulled back hard on the rod with all of his strength. The fish was clearly winning this first tug of war as line slipped off the reel in spite of his strong double thumb death grip against the spool of Dacron line. Quickly he reeled the line tight one last time, as I yelled my final request.

"*Now*, hit him one more time with all you've got."

He pulled back on the rod with all of his might still unable to prevent more line from leaving the reel.

"Good job. You're doing great!"

As he dropped into my fighting chair, his wife was asked to stand behind it and concentrate on pointing him directly toward the fish at all times. It was time to let the games begin.

HE WATCHED HELPLESSLY as more and more of the Dacron line peeled off the reel and disappeared over the stern with alarming speed.

"Not to worry. Eventually he will stop his first run or we'll start the boat and chase him."

I was elated to know we had a good strong fish hooked up, but I was also privately worried that I would have to simultaneously wear the three hats of captain, mate, and coach. I would somehow have to get the three of us to work together as a complete team in order to capture this fish, whatever it turned out to be!

Finally the long first run stopped, and I began encouraging my excited new shark fisherman to use short, pumping strokes to regain line. When I looked at the reel spool, it was clear that the fish had removed approximately half of the 750 yards of Dacron line in his initial run. An impressive opening gambit on his part, to say the least!

"Pace yourself, because this battle has only just begun," I said.

I didn't want to tell him that I knew from the initial run he had his hands full with this fish. As he pumped and reeled, his wife continued to point him at the fish by turning the fighting chair. She had her job down pat, and I had at least one less thing to worry about.

After fifteen or twenty minutes of alternately retrieving and losing line, the fish began to slowly circle the boat about one hundred yards away. I jumped up to the controls on the command bridge, started both engines, and used the clutches to slowly spin the boat away from the fish. This action effectively kept the shark positioned off the stern where we could continue to safely do battle.

After close to an hour of continuous loss and retrieval of line while repeatedly spinning the boat, the fifty feet of 130-pound test Dacron that was spliced on to the end of the 80-pound line began to show. In a few minutes we would finally be able to see the fish. Following a few more pulls by the now tired angler, I grabbed the leader and told him to slack off slightly on the drag. The shadow of an immense shark began to rise into view from the depths of the sixty-foot water. I found the fish was much too strong to be controlled on the leader. It was just not possible to pull it the last twenty feet to the boat.

"I can finally see your fish. It appears to be a very large dusky shark about eleven feet long!"

He looked at me in amazement. "What's a dusky shark?"

"It's a magnificent fish to battle, but one that is extremely strong and not even beginning to tire yet. You're going to have to hang tough and continue to pace yourself."

As I finished my statement, the shark must have seen the boat because he started to pull with a new vengeance, and I was powerless to stop him even though I was holding the leader with both hands and bracing myself against the stern coaming with my thighs. I quickly dropped the leader back in the water and shouted.

"Get ready to hold on. Slowly retighten the drag!"

The great shark dove into the depths.

MY GUEST WAS SWEATING PROFUSELY and tiring in the intense heat, so I instructed him to alternately release his right arm and then his left arm from the rod so he could rest and stretch his now aching biceps. The fighting harness he was wearing took the weight of the rod and the fish while he did this. He also managed to rest a bit while we waited for the fish to complete each steady, determined run away from the boat. As time passed, we brought the huge fish to within fifteen to twenty feet of the boat nine more times. Each time the fish was more tired but was certainly far from rolling on his side in submission. I looked at my angler—he was starting to show signs of exhaustion, muscle cramping, and possible early stage heat exhaustion. In spite of the size and strength of the man I had in the fighting chair, the fish clearly had the upper hand. It appeared the fish was going to win the battle as it was only a matter of time before he would totally exhaust the angler. Consequently, I decided we needed a new approach to whip this powerful dusky shark. I thought about putting his wife in the chair for a while. No, that would be a bad idea because her husband would never really be able to say he caught this powerful creature by himself! In the annals of sport fishing there is no glory or pride in a catch if someone else takes a turn in the fight.

I needed to encourage both of them. "Aha! I know how to beat this fish before you run out of energy. If you can give me about fifteen more gutsy minutes of cranking, we'll conquer this monster."

My idea was quite simple, and I must give credit where credit is due. John Thurston, undoubtedly the best shark fisherman in the state of Virginia, shared this trick at one of the meetings of the Virginia Beach Sharkers. I told the almost defeated angler to give the fish everything he had so I could grab the leader one more time. While he struggled to bring the fish near again, I rigged up my larger 12/0 rod and reel and left the terminal snap swivel in an open position. Once he cranked the leader tip to the boat, I would clip the 12/0 rig into the swivel attached to the leader and then we could fight the fish on a more even playing field. Simple, yet brilliant. The plan depended on split second timing, the fish cooperating long enough, and my angler having a short burst of strength. We really had no other choice if we wanted to capture this fish.

One more time he grunted and strained to pump the huge fish up toward the boat. Ever so slowly the leader tip approached the side of the boat. I already had the end of the 12/0 rig in my right hand and reached for the approaching leader with my left hand by leaning over the gunwale as far as I safely could. My plan was to quickly clip in the new leader, and then I hoped to have time to unclip the smaller 9/0 before the fish got up a new head of steam and charged off again. *Snap—clip!* The 12/0 rig was now attached to the swivel at the end of the leader.

Immediately I turned and yelled, "Lock your thumbs down hard!"

As he did this, I managed to squeeze hard on the 9/0 leader's 500-pound coast lock swivel to unclip it and remove it from the hook rig.

"Clear!" I yelled. "Hand me your pole and grab the 12/0 rod from your wife."

Once he had the stronger 12/0 rod in his hands, I knew we had the upper hand against the shark. Now charges away from the boat became less frequent and covered shorter distances. As he pumped and reeled, the fish finally showed signs of tiring.

AFTER SPINNING THE BOAT in a circle one last time, we finally had the fish lying on its side next to the boat. In spite of the shark's momentarily docile appearance, it was time to again remind my charters of the need for safety at the end game. I carefully laid the open noose of my half-inch nylon tail rope on the deck and asked my determined angler to slack off his drag, get out of the fighting chair, and stand in the middle of the noose.

Quickly I worked the noose up and over his body and rod tip, down the leader, and gently over the shark's head. I then used the end of a tagging stick to gently ease the noose first over the dorsal fin and then over each pectoral fin while keeping a close eye on the shark. Meanwhile the angler, who had already placed his rod in a forward rod holder so he could grab it quickly if necessary, was dutifully holding on to the leader.

We were now at the moment of truth. I had secured one end of the tail rope to a stern cleat, knowing this would force the fish to pull the 16,000 pound boat if I was not successful in snatching up the looped end of the tail rope fast enough and tight enough.

Here we go! I said to myself. As I leaned over the side and gently slid the tail rope toward the shark's scythe-like tail, I used both hands to rapidly close the noose. As the noose came tight against the shark's tail, I was already lifting myself back up over the gunwale and down to the stern cleat where I took two quick turns, leaned back on the deck, and used my body weight to help secure the rope against the cleat. I let the boat and the cleat take the brunt of the shark's efforts to surge away and twist and writhe as he tried to get free. No way would we lose this fish now. We had done it! Both charter guests were now asked to hold the first line while I worked a second tail rope over the fish and secured it with several reverse wraps to take the strain.

I then shook hands with my relieved husband-and-wife team and congratulated them on catching a trophy-size shark. With only the three of us, it would be impossible to pull the shark over the three-foot-high gunwales because we simply did not have the muscle power on board to do it. Since I did not want to spend hours towing the large fish to port, I decided to use a come-a-long to winch it through the transom door. Once the fish settled down and stopped thrashing against the boat, I walked it slowly from the stern cleat to the transom door, keeping his tail well out of the water. No way would I chance losing this fish after the ordeal my angler had been through to catch it.

When I got the shark's tail into the opening of the transom door, I secured a come-a-long with its cable and hook to a forward pad eye. The other end terminated in a short loop that fit over the shark's tail. The three of us then began taking turns cranking the shark into the boat a few inches at a time, and ever so slowly the great fish inched into the cockpit. The cable on the come-a-long was taut with tremendous strain, and I warned my guests not to stand directly in line with the angle of pull in case anything broke loose.

After forty minutes, the shark was two-thirds of the way through the cockpit door and immobile on the deck from his own immense weight. The shark would go no farther as its two pectoral fins anchored it against the transom while the large girth wedged it firmly in the cockpit door opening, preventing it from moving any further into the boat. The menacing head was now out of the water resting on the boat's swim platform. All that remained was to remove the rope from the come-a-long and attach additional tail ropes securely to both stern cleats.

IT WOULD BE A PLEASURE to run *Ocean Venture* in at planing speed rather than tow the fish at three or four knots for several hours. I restarted the engines and aimed the bow southwest toward Rudee Inlet as cold sodas were opened all around. An exhausted but victorious angler was relaxing on the port seat, watching the shark for any signs of movement.

Suddenly, in a very tired but excited voice, he asked two questions. "How big do you think this fish is, and what kind of a shark did you say it is?"

After a moment's thought I answered his questions. "It is probably over four hundred pounds and is definitely a dusky shark."

He sat quietly absorbing my pronouncement as we headed steadily toward the beach. The enormity of what he had just accomplished was beginning to sink in.

As we slowed down at the entrance to Rudee Inlet, I gazed sideways at the jetty fishermen knowing our "stern" passenger's large girth and toothy jaw wedged in the open transom door would attract immediate attention and comments. Sure enough, the jetty anglers were pointing and announcing our arrival. Several of them poked their companions if they were not looking in our direction.

"Look at the size of that shark!"

Many on the jetty gave us the thumbs up sign as we idled slowly past them.

Miraculously the fatigue we were all feeling was now starting to lessen in view of these friendly angling accolades.

I knew we would be all set at the weigh-in dock at Fisherman's Wharf Marina as I had radioed ahead for clearance. Normally there is a charter boat moored at the weigh-in scale location, but since it was only mid-afternoon, that boat was still out with its charter, leaving us clear access to the scales.

When we got to the dock, a good-sized crowd of onlookers, including some tourists, had already gathered. I knew this would be both good and bad. Good that we would have all the volunteer manpower we would need in hoisting and weighing the large shark but bad that we would be subject to a predictable barrage of questions. Sure enough, no sooner had I tied off *Ocean Venture* to the dock, the inevitable questions began from the gathering crowd of curious tourists.

"Where did you catch that big shark?"

"What was the bait?"

"Which one of you caught it? Was it the lady?"

"What kind of rod and reel did you use?"

"How big is your boat?"

"How much did your boat cost?"

I did not have time to answer all of these questions as the weigh master had already passed me a rope for readying the shark for the scale.

I slipped a weighing loop of rope over the shark's tail and began to rig it for lifting and weighing with the dock's block and tackle while seven of the men on the dock quickly responded to a request to help with the lifting rope. More questions then resumed.

"How long did it take to catch it?"

"How much do you think it will weigh?"

This last question was one I had learned some time ago not to answer publicly, even if I had a pretty good idea. I always deferred to the weigh master. I glanced at the day's angler, however, and could see he was enjoying this new and strange form of notoriety.

I repeatedly warned the men who were volunteering to help lift the fish to stay well away from it. I never fully trusted a lifting rig not to give way. A shark's teeth and skin can do a lot of damage even if the fish is dead.

After much coordinated pulling and heaving, the fish was suspended upside down totally off the ground. The men were then told to lower it slightly onto the steel hook attached to the scales. The dock weigh-master came out of his air-conditioned office, climbed the platform to the scale, and began moving the counter weights slowly to find the balance point for the fish. Finally he boomed out the much awaited numbers. "**Four twenty-seven!**"

As a first-time shark angler, my raffle winner had just caught one of the best dusky sharks of the season and had reason to be quite proud of himself. The two of us then followed the weigh-master into his office so the fish could be registered for a Virginia Saltwater Tournament citation plaque. The shark was two hundred seventy-seven pounds heavier than the one hundred fifty-pound required minimum citation weight.

When we returned to my slip at Lynnhaven Waterway Marina, my anglers departed exhausted but ecstatic. As I drove home after sunset, I thought to myself, *In spite of not having a mate, I still had a helluva good day on the water.*

THE FINAL CHAPTER of this fishing trip actually occurred when I attended the next meeting of the Virginia Beach Sharkers. Word must have spread by telephone as to the result of my one-man charter for the club's raffle winner. I remember getting a huge round of applause as I walked into the meeting room. Yes, it made me feel good as an angler and a teacher of fishermen. I was sure to thank one of my mentors, John Thurston, for sharing his end game rod switching technique so that I could find "another way to skin the cat."

Captain's Tip: Being young and naïve, I and many other sharkers believed that catching and not releasing large sharks was acceptable. How wrong we were! In a few short years I came to my senses and began tagging and releasing all the sharks caught from my boats. Research has shown that sharks are slow growing, need many years to reach sexual maturity, and often have small numbers of offspring. All this did not bode well for the fishery. Sure enough, after excessive commercial and recreational pressure on the shark stock throughout the 1980s, their numbers, as evidenced by catch statistics, are on a serious decline. So please, if you are lucky enough to hook one of these beautiful fish, take a picture, insert a tag, and release it to fight and breed another day!

10

A Fish Far Too Big

IN MY ESTIMATION, October in southeast Virginia is one of the nicest months of the year. It is also one of the best times to be out on the open waters of the Chesapeake Bay. The water is still quite warm as it is slow to lose all the heat energy it has absorbed from the scorching, sultry days of our Tidewater summers. The air is usually pleasantly warm, in the high 60s to low 70s, after the morning chill and dew have burned off.

On one such particular October day in the 1980s, my wife, Nancy, who has been fishing with me for the past forty years, agreed to accompany me for a relaxing day of bay flounder fishing. As we cleared the inlet, she helped me keep a lookout for the ever-present crab pots, floating debris, and other boats.

"What is that gray object ahead? It looks like a small submarine," Nancy said when we were less than half a mile from the inlet entrance.

I saw no such vessel as I peered ahead. "Where do you see a submarine?"

"Look over there about ten degrees off the starboard bow," my wife replied.

As we were going about thirty knots, I slowed the boat down and tried to focus on the near horizon of the Thimble Shoals shipping channel. This was the only place a submarine could be without running aground. I *really* hoped my wife was mistaken. Unnoticed, even at a relatively low speed in the harbor or bay, submarines normally displace enough water to put out a huge bow wave that can easily swamp a small boat like my twenty-four-footer or wreak havoc with a boat and its occupants. Their huge bow waves can be particularly dangerous on a calm day when you would least expect them.

To my exasperation, there was still no submarine anywhere in my field of view. "Are you sure you are not looking further out toward the Baltimore shipping channel?" The channel was about nine miles from us.

"No, Mike. Try looking closer to the boat on the line of bearing I gave you."

Suddenly I thought I saw something about one mile from us that appeared to be the color of a submarine, but it would be way out of the shipping channel.

"I think I see it, but I don't believe it is a submarine. Let's head over there and look."

As we approached the area, we could both see geysers of water shooting up in the air intermittently. Once we got even closer, it quickly became apparent that Nancy had picked out a large whale. A whale in the bay! It was an awe-inspiring as well as unusual sight. As we slowly idled closer and closer, the whale seemed to be about thirty to thirty-five feet long. As it rolled on its side, it beat the water with a twelve-foot-long pectoral fin. We stopped the boat a respectful distance away and silently watched the playful mammal.

As best we could determine, it was some type of juvenile whale that seemed to be stunning its prey by smacking the water violently with its pectoral fin and then enjoying its catch. The ultimate fisherman! Mesmerized we just sat there for a good twenty or thirty minutes watching the whale feed. There were no other human beings or boats in sight.

Eventually when another fishing boat started to charge up toward us, we waved at him to slow down and veer off. We really did not want him to disturb the whale or the wonderful scene we were watching. Once he realized it was a whale, the fisherman didn't seem to care as he gunned his motor and rocketed off in pursuit of whatever fish he was seeking for the day. Not us. This was an experience of a lifetime worth trading for a hundred fishing trips. We stayed and marveled as long as the whale let us.

From our early boating trips on Long Island Sound to surf fishing on the Outer Banks of North Carolina to more recent pier fishing on the east and west coasts of Florida, my wife and I have shared several unusual experiences. This was one of those special moments that God occasionally provides us, and I was glad to share the enjoyment of it with my wife.

After we had our fill of whale watching, we headed toward the Chesapeake Bay Bridge Tunnel to continue our fishing trip. Unfortunately we would have to work harder than the whale to catch our dinner! The tide was just starting out, and we were glad we had lots of lively minnows and squid for bait. I always prefer the outgoing tide in the fall because the bay and creek waters are warmer and tend to sweep bait out toward the mouth of the bay. As Nancy resumed steering the boat, I took the rods and attached several flounder rigs I knew would produce fish for us. I am partial to green buck tail rigs with reflective Mylar strips. One of fishing's long time sayings comes to mind: *If it ain't chartreuse, it ain't no use!* Each hook was tipped with a triangular squid pennant coupled with a very lively bull-gudgeon minnow. By the time we reached the eight-mile post of the bridge tunnel, four chartreuse terminal rigs were already baited up with six-ounce sinkers attached and were ready to lower to the bottom. This area was a bonanza of small mini-plateaus and holes that always seemed to hold schools of flounder.

Nancy and I spent the next several hours drifting away from the tunnel, picking up several flounder per drift. Following each drift, we would motor back to the eight-mile post and begin the ritual again. Once the four lures were bouncing along the bottom, we had the option of leaving all of them in the rod holders or actively fishing them. Nancy preferred to leave hers in the rod holders so she could relax. Unbelievably, she still managed to out fish me while I actively worked one of the rods. Her laid back approach resulted in initial taps eventually turning into recurring yanks on the rod as a flounder would work his way up from the back end of her bait and finally impale himself on the Kahle hook. However, I always think it is better to be able to drop the lure back to these fish as they bite their way up from the back of the bait toward the hook. I guess when they are hungry enough in the fall, prior to migration, they will pretty much hook themselves!

Since the afternoon sea breeze had strengthened from the northeast and we had a cooler of delicious flounder, it was time to head in. Nancy drove the boat while I scrubbed the cockpit. That way, all we had to do was rinse the rest of the boat when we got back to the dock. By now the windswept waves were topped with whitecaps and steadily building in size as my wife picked up speed and left the first island of the Chesapeake Bay Bridge Tunnel in *Ocean Venture's* wake. In between the whitecaps ahead, she noticed a small overturned catamaran with two sailors clinging perilously to one of the hulls.

"Mike, there is a Hobie Cat between us and the beach that has turned over in the water. Should we stop and see if they need help?"

"Of course. They will never get the boat back up on their own in this brisk wind. Let me go below and find that large tow rope we have."

Nancy began to steer toward the distressed boaters while keeping me informed of what was happening. I could hear her through the companionway but could not see what she was looking at. I was unsuccessfully rummaging in each cabin locker looking for the fifty-foot nylon line I had stowed for just such a need. My wife chimed in with an update.

"There are two men in full wet suits in the water. They are hanging on to a line trying to use their body weight to pull the catamaran back up. They are not having any luck. I think the wind is too strong for them."

"Okay, Nancy, slow down and motor up to them while I find this tow line."

As *Ocean Venture* approached the two sailors, Nancy called out to them, "Would you two like some help? I can throw you a line and use the boat to pull your Hobie Cat upright for you."

Still in the cabin, I did not hear an immediate response. Then the voices I heard from beyond the stern were not making my wife very happy.

"Do you think she has any clue about what to do to help us?" yelled one of the sailors above the sound of the wind.

"Is she the only one on the boat? I'm not sure if we should let her help us or not."

"If we don't let her help, we might not get the boat righted and get back to shore."

"Have you ever seen a woman running a twin-throttle sportfisherman alone before?"

As the distant dialogue continued, I glanced up the companionway at my wife and could read anger written all over her face. Finally, I had my hands on the line I was after.

"Nancy, I found it! Let's go help those two out."

"I don't think they appreciate the help that is here." My wife's next comment floored me. "They sound like a pair of male chauvinists, and I'd like to leave them here. We don't need to spend the extra time it will take to help them!"

She was really angry! Once I got back up on deck, it took some serious discussion to convince my wife that these two jerks needed to be helped. When they saw me come up on deck, the two of them looked suddenly relieved. After a very short discussion, they sheepishly told us they would gladly accept our help.

As I threw them the tow line, my wife was continuing to fume. Once we used the engines to right their sailboat, the two sailors climbed back on board and actually thanked us.

As we returned to the inlet, Nancy was still muttering, "Should have towed their boat to shore and left both of them to wash out of the bay with the tide! Maybe they would have learned some manners and respect."

All in all, even with the sailboat adventure, we had an outstanding day. Not only did we have plenty of fat two- to four-pound flounder to clean, but we had helped some fellow mariners and been privileged to observe one of nature's most unique creatures in the wild.

AS THE YEARS WENT ON, I gradually discovered that our whale sighting was not quite as rare as I thought. There have actually been other moments where I have encountered whales either in the bay or just off shore from Virginia Beach. November is also a good month for spotting whales. At the northern end of the Chesapeake Bay Bridge Tunnel there is a North Channel that runs under the High Level Bridge and then up the bay toward Baltimore, including a stretch that is as deep as one hundred thirty feet. One November while striper and flounder fishing, my boating buddies and I were treated to the sight of a good-sized whale swimming and feeding in this channel. The whale was inside the bridge tunnel close to Fisherman's Island and quite at ease being so close to land.

I have come very close to whales when I have run up on them unexpectedly just off Cape Henry in the deeper seventy- to eighty-foot water in late November and early December. It is quite startling to come upon one of these whales in the deeper water when they have just breached without any forewarning. Frequently they will come up suddenly with their mouth wide open in a feeding action that is termed "lunch feeding." In most cases they are feeding on bay anchovies and small menhaden.

EACH WHALE EXPERIENCE has been remarkable and a completely unique encounter. Humpback, fin, and occasionally right whales continue to make their presence known off Virginia Beach in December, January, February, and March. These whales are generally young adults in the thirty- to fifty-foot size range and are most frequently found from the waters directly off Cape Henry to approximately five miles south of Rudee Inlet. Locals and visitors without boats have the opportunity to view them occasionally from the shore and, more predictably, from large, comfortable head boats. The boats leave from Rudee Inlet on designated whale watching trips. In many cases there is a marine interpreter from the Virginia Aquarium on board the boat to both narrate and answer questions. The aquarium or the Rudee Inlet Fishing Center is a good starting point to plan one of these outings.

Captain's Tip: Take the time to enjoy the ocean's greatest creature if you come across a whale while on the water or take a whale watching boat trip. You will not regret the decision!

Federal whale watching regulations generally restrict the viewing distance for most whales to a minimum of three hundred yards and as much as five hundred yards for a restricted species, such as right whales. So do keep a respectful distance if in your own boat as whales are protected marine mammals and should not be disturbed. This distance will also afford a degree of safety in case of a breach. You should also not change speed or direction while observing whales. Whales are quite sensitive to changes in noise they have become accustomed to and can become frightened by the sudden disappearance of a noise, such as your boat engine, just as well as by any sudden unexpected noise. It is best to slow to idle speed or a stop and let your engines idle for at least a minute before shutting them off. Similarly, when leaving the observation area, idle away slowly and get some appreciable distance between you and the whales before pushing the throttles and planing the boat at higher speed.

11

Riding Shotgun For A Monster Shark

I REMEMBER that extraordinary fishing day just as clearly now, twenty-seven years later, as when it unfolded on a hot night in late July 1981. My former student Craig Paige and I were at it again, entered in the annual Virginia Beach Shark Tournament sponsored by our club. There were numerous prizes up for grabs for the winners. More importantly, however, we were probably drawn most by the challenge of the immense competition and the potential thrill from catching a really big shark.

The first day of the tournament had resulted in a really rough ride out into the Atlantic. We had to fight three- and four-foot seas all the way from the mouth of the bay. It was so rough for my nineteen-foot Bayliner that we actually followed a freighter out of the Chesapeake Bay to let it break the seas for us most of the way out into the ocean. Due to the very rough weather, we settled on fishing an area not quite as far as we would have preferred.

Craig and I had fished hard all day and were dog tired, having started by fighting the seas at 5:00 A.M. before the sun had risen. In the very late afternoon, after a long slow day with absolutely no hits or run-offs, we were ready to quit fishing and head to the dock for hot food and a shower. Craig, however, convinced me to pull in the dead stingray I was using for bait, make some deep slits in it, and toss it back in the ocean for one last try. That was a move I shall never regret. Within fifteen minutes I had a strong, steady pull on the clicker of my 9/0 shark rig and prepared to set the hook hard several times. Once struck, the fish I had hooked ran off an initial two hundred plus yards.

That in itself was not unusual, even from some of the larger brown sharks that we had caught. What was unusual was that after the first run off, it was almost impossible to gain any line on this fish. He pulled like a tank in low gear with a rope attached. It could best be described as a hard fought tug-of-war. However, for the first hour, it was more like he tugged and I felt any hard earned line get pulled back out.

Meanwhile, while I was struggling to gain line, Craig excitedly had grabbed the VHF radio and called for a tournament committee boat.

"Any committee boat, this is *Drifter* and we are hooked up! This is one tough fish, so it might be a while before we arrive at the dock. Over."

"*Drifter*, we read you loud and clear. Since you are hooked up, take as long as you need to boat the fish. Good luck."

The shark refused to show himself for the entire first hour. After losing the first hour of the tug-of-war, I started to concentrate on my pumping and reeling technique. This was most difficult work as there was no fighting chair on *Drifter*, and the best I could do was sit on the motor box, hold the rod butt in the gimbal of the fighting belt I was wearing, and brace my feet against the side of the boat. I worked at taking very short drops with the rod tip so I could finally start to regain some of the 80-pound Dacron line. Craig lent encouragement as he watched me continuously pull and strain as the fish remained in control. There was no doubt at this point that the shark had really swallowed the stingray and was solidly attached to at least one of the two 14/0 hooks on my hook rig. The hook was definitely not coming out. Either he would lose or I would get whipped.

For the next hour and a half this fish was determined to wear me out. By periodically resting one arm at a time and shaking the cramps out, I was equally determined not to let him rest but so long. As the sun started to dip toward the western horizon, the tide of battle finally started to turn in our direction. I welcomed the relief because I did not have much more energy left.

Right before sunset, the fish surfaced and showed us the classic profile of a dusky shark. He had clearly been using his two enormous pectoral fins to push against the water in a valiant effort to stay far from the boat. After walking me around the boat several times, we could tell he was quite tired. I pressured the line to work him to the side of the boat for tail roping, and by now I was definitely more fatigued than the fish. Once Craig attempted to tail rope the shark, I vividly remember that shark rearing back with his long tail and striking Craig extremely hard in an area where we guys hate to be hit. I believe that the gimbal harness Craig was still wearing probably managed to save him from some serious injury from that lethal tail. Once we finally got an initial tail rope on the fish, we secured him with additional half-inch lines and called in on the VHF radio to report that we would be bringing in a fish for weighing.

Between the two of us, our joint end game efforts had paid off handsomely as we were both now looking at a good-sized shark securely tail roped to my port stern cleat. We guessed it was at least four hundred pounds and was a dusky shark, which explained why it had fought so hard. Dusky sharks are notorious for long protracted battles with little loss of their strength while the angler's energy wears down. At least we now had a chance to place in the tournament!

DURING THE FIGHT and its conclusion, the sun had slowly dipped below the horizon, and we were now enjoying the calm of a beautiful summer twilight. Together we stowed and straightened our gear and prepared to make the inevitable long slow tow back to Rudee Inlet to weigh our fish. With only two of us in the boat, we could never pull a shark of this size over the gunwale, hence the long trip to the dock. We were both ready to return to dry land and a good hot meal.

"Craig, do you mind running the boat as I am *really* whipped?"

"I don't mind at all. Why don't you watch the shark and the lines while we head in."

From my earlier experiences pitching a full game of baseball in college, I knew the fatigue and muscle soreness I was experiencing would get worse. Within a few minutes, darkness began to descend on the now calm seas and we proceeded to rely on the compass for our heading. Each of us peered intently into the distance for the appearance of the bright lights of the hotels on the Virginia Beach oceanfront resort strip. Once we got closer to the beach we knew we could shift our focus to the jetty light for safely navigating Rudee Inlet. That last part of the trip would require constant navigation concentration as the Rudee Inlet entrance can be treacherous due to shoaling, only one bright beacon, and an *extremely* narrow channel. This would be a *very* slow trip at maybe three or four miles per hour with our newly acquired finned friend slowing us down with his massive drag as we towed him tail first backward through the water.

As I sat down with a cold drink in the seat next to Craig, I heard a radio call on Channel 68. "This is *Relentless* calling any Virginia Beach Sharkers still out fishing."

I immediately picked up the microphone and responded, "*Relentless*, this is *Drifter*, over."

A reply came right back. "*Drifter*, this is *Relentless*. I am on a course headed toward Rudee Inlet and am still a good twenty miles off the beach. I have virtually no steerageway or ability to maneuver as I have in tow one of the largest sharks I have ever caught. Are you in a position to assist, over?"

This was fellow club member, former president, and all-around good guy John Thurston. John was without a doubt the premier shark fisherman in the state of Virginia. John and his long-time fishing partner Bill Moffett were coming in from offshore about ten miles behind us. Of course we would help!

"John, this is Mike Halperin and Craig Paige, what do you need us to do?"

"*Drifter*, as you approach the shipping lanes, can you give me a heads up if there are any ships or freighters headed northbound or southbound down the beach. I will be unable to avoid them and may need to stop with my tow until they pass."

"*Relentless*, we've got your back. Will call you and keep you posted on any shipping we see."

Now that John had brought this issue up, I was secretly hoping we would not encounter any Navy ships or freighters on our own as our speed and ability to maneuver was also quite limited. John was a lot worse off than we were as he seemed to have a much larger fish in tow. Both of our little fiberglass boats moving at only two or three knots would have no chance to avoid a north or southbound freighter or naval vessel traveling at anywhere from fifteen to twenty-five or more knots. Our only hope would be either clear passage through the shipping lanes or enough notice to stop temporarily if necessary. As the night wore on, the two freighters we sighted and reported to *Relentless* passed harmlessly south a good distance in front of us. After about two hours, we were finally able to make our way through Rudee Inlet and to the Fisherman's Wharf weigh station. As we approached the rock jetties, I called *Relentless* on the radio and told John that he was now on his own for the rest of the trip in.

"Thank you, guys, for your help. I'll see you at the dock in about an hour."

WHEN WE ARRIVED AT THE DOCK and tied up the boat, it was already late at night and a large crowd had already gathered. The crowd wanted to see the sharks weighed in and see the standings on the tournament leader board. Apparently the standings were changing constantly as late arrivers kept besting previous catches from the day. Fortunately we were in that group as my dusky shark weighed in at 555 ½ pounds! Unfortunately for us, this was to be a banner year for our tournament, and my fish was only big enough to eventually earn fifth place when all the weigh-ins were over. Still, this would place for a prize, a brand new 6/0 Penn reel.

A lot of excitement had started to build over John Thurston's catch. While talking on the radio, he had shared that he and Bill Moffett had had to secure several additional tail ropes as the weight of his fish kept breaking his tow ropes on the way in. The radio had been abuzz on channel 68 about these problems and how he needed our "eyes and ears" in front of him to avoid a calamity with coastal shipping.

When *Relentless* finally pulled up to the weigh station, the dock was mobbed with people. It was a mixture of Virginia Beach Sharkers and tourists who were enjoying the show. Some of the tourists worried those of us in the club near the weighing station. Even though the club had roped off the weigh-in area, several people kept pressing closer and closer in an attempt to touch some of the sharks or see them up close. What they did not realize was that some of these large fish might not be completely dead even after a long trip to the dock. Occasionally captured sharks were known to snap their jaws involuntarily in some type of post-mortem reflex. Club members were trying to keep the tourists back while some of the teenagers and even a few of the adults would try anything to be able to say they had touched one of the sharks. After they were weighed, the sharks were lined up on the dock for examination by VIMS. The Virginia Institute of Marine Science is an outstanding marine research facility in Gloucester that scientifically studied the sharks brought in each year in our tournaments. The information they gathered would add to their research about Atlantic shark populations.

IN THIS SULTRY SUMMER NIGHT circus atmosphere, the tail of John Thurston's shark was finally placed on the short double-loop line that would ultimately attach it to the steel hook for the weighing scales. Nine or ten of the Virginia Beach Sharkers volunteered to hoist the shark from the boat to the scale so it could hang free and be weighed. It was near midnight and completely dark except for some of the floodlights at the fishing center. The shark loomed larger as each segment of its body slowly and surrealistically emerged from behind John's center console boat. The shark rose tail first from below the bulkhead as lots of club members pulled on the block and tackle rope in unison. With each pull more of the massive girth of John's shark began to emerge into the light. Finally the distinct square snout and jaw of a massive tiger shark cleared the edge of the bulkhead. At that moment, a great collective gasp and multiple shouts of approval came from the crowd. Even prior to weighing, it was clear that John had caught one colossal tiger shark! Finally, the fish steadied full weight on the scales and the weigh-master spoke.

"One thousand ninety-nine pounds and twelve ounces!"

Applause and cheers sprang up everywhere from the people present.

In one day of fishing John had not only won the 1981 Virginia Beach Shark Tournament, but had shattered the record for the largest fish ever caught in Virginia with a new state record tiger shark! This was clearly a great night for John and a tremendous night for the Virginia Beach Sharkers and sportfishing in Virginia Beach. As I write this twenty-seven years later, no one has even come close to beating John Thurston's record fish. Craig and I felt privileged to have contributed in a small way by riding "shotgun" and assisting John's safe arrival to the dock on this memorable day of fishing.

Captain's Tip: There are not always many other boaters to assist anglers out on the water. Always take every opportunity to help out a fellow angler, and the favor will probably be returned in kind some day.

Captain's Note: With the current state of the oceanic shark fishery, it is quite possible that no one will ever break this particular Virginia state record. Commercial long-line fishing by U.S. and foreign boats has severely reduced the size and number of sharks in our coastal stocks, particularly the larger fish that take many years to reach maturity and trophy size. At the time, however, the Sharkers club could not have foreseen this pending marked decline in the world's shark population. Sadly, the Sharkers disbanded as a club a few years after this event.

By Bob Hutchinson

John W. Thurston Jr. and record-smashing tiger shark.

Angler Surprised By Record Shark

Reprinted with permission of the Virginian-Pilot.

12
The Most Regal of Fish

FEW FISH hold the angling mystique of the fabled striped bass. Perhaps this legendary status dates to the time of their discovery as an abundant food resource in American colonial times, or maybe it is because of their anadromous status from birth in fresh water streams and rivers to their migratory lives in saltwater, where they grow to rod breaking proportions and prowl the roughest of waters. Certainly they are high on every angler's desirable "catch" list due to their regal appearance and excellent taste.

In Virginia Beach and the adjacent Chesapeake Bay, we are fortunate to have a true melting pot for stripers. Here stripers that have left river systems and actively spent the summer feeding in the northeast return in the fall to co-mingle with a local population of striped bass. The fish that have remained in our bay have usually not reached sexual maturity and are often referred to as "resident fish." This situation provides a true rockfish bonanza for Chesapeake Bay anglers. Trophy-size striped bass are normally first available beginning in March until they finish spawning and exit the bay a few weeks later. The hunt for these larger stripers resumes again later in the year when large schools that have followed the bait north return to our area in November and December. A percentage of these winter trophy fish also owe their origin to river systems in the northeast. As long as schools of menhaden linger along the Virginia Beach coast, the larger stripers normally remain in our near offshore waters often through January, February, and even into March. Following the seasonal March-April push of spawning stripers up the bay's rivers, we are left with a steady population of smaller school-size rockfish that keep us busy catching stripers even during Virginia's summertime catch and release period.

For many of us, smaller school-sized stripers garner our attention when they devour live spot during the summer and fall that were intended for trophy-size flounder. This frequently occurs in July, August, and September when fishing directly over the tubes of the Chesapeake Bay Bridge Tunnel. With Virginia's fall striper season not opening now until early October, it has been obligatory to release these fat, healthy eating-size striped bass. For someone who likes to fish "peaks," I normally wait until late October and November to target these fish in earnest. I much prefer November to October because schools of stripers can usually be found in vast expanses of open bay water away from the structure of the seventeen-mile long Chesapeake Bay Bridge Tunnel. This avoids having to worry about snagging tunnel pilings or competing with the scores of boats trolling along the tunnel.

* * * *

One November day during striper season, John Reinhardt, Nancy, and I headed out in *Ocean Venture* to troll for stripers. Nancy and I always thoroughly enjoyed John's companionship. Not only was he a good friend and good company, but he was also a Renaissance man. As a talented musician and operatic tenor, he was always embarking on special musical projects, including writing children's operas. He is also well known in the Tidewater area for his past performances with the Tidewater Winds. Since we both shared naval military backgrounds and a true passion for fishing, conversation during our outings was always stimulating and enjoyable.

AT THE CORE OF OUR PURSUIT of stripers, binoculars and the depth (fish) finder always serve as our best tools in locating fish. Binoculars are perfect for spotting seagulls actively diving to the surface of the water. This diving is a sure sign that a school of fish is feeding on something below the surface, leaving lots of tasty scraps to float up and attract the birds. Occasionally it is a school of bluefish, but in most instances it is striped bass. Once the three of us spotted a group of working birds, we raced to the spot, slowed down, and then patiently circled the edges checking the depth finder. When we marked large clouds of baitfish with some larger blips on the Raytheon sonar, we dropped our two trolling rigs in.

Because of the need to feel everything happening on the business end of the lures, I normally fish with 50-pound braided line or 40-pound stainless wire line. No matter what line I use, it is spooled on a Penn 320 level-wind graphite reel attached to a medium weight trolling rod with a very sensitive tip. Each rod has Aftco roller guides for ease of line handling under pressure. In water shallower than thirty feet, sometimes I troll using just monofilament line.

For starter baits on the first two rods, we ran six-inch chartreuse curly tail grubs attached to 1/8 ounce white bucktail jigs with 7/0 hooks. If there were stripers around the bait school we had seen below us, we would find out real fast. Since we were in open water, we streamed these rigs back from the stern rod holders, let the sinkers hit bottom, and let out a few more turns of line so the sinkers would continue to bounce bottom as we idled along slowly. This enabled the lures to work their magic just two or three feet above the bottom of the bay where the stripers were most likely to be prowling. A three-way swivel at the end of the trolling line allowed us to position our bucktails in the "strike zone." One arm of the swivel was attached by three feet of monofilament to a twelve-ounce teardrop sinker. The second arm had twenty-five feet of Ande monofilament tied directly to the lure itself with a loop knot that allowed the lure to dance enticingly.

The last rig was a short, 5'2" custom standup trolling rod, also with a Penn 320 reel and a pistol grip. On this rig's terminal gear, we ran a plain white 1/8 ounce bucktail with a 7/0 hook and a piece of Uncle Josh's #70 yellow pork rind as a trailer on the hook. This rod I always fished actively in my hand so I could not only jig it back and forth but also feel the bottom to see if the amount of line out needed to be adjusted.

Within moments of dropping these rigs to the bottom, we had an immediate strong hit. The rod in the port side stern rod holder bent over almost double as its clicker announced the slow release of line to an unhappy fish.

"John!" I yelled. "Grab that rod quickly before we lose any more line off the reel. I think you have a nice striper on the other end!"

With the enormous stress the fish was putting on the rod, I watched as John struggled to remove the rod from the holder.

"Can you slow the boat down so I can get this rod out of the holder?" John asked Nancy.

"She needs to maintain *some* forward motion or we'll risk losing the fish, John. Try slowly wiggling the rod butt back and forth as you try to pull it out."

That technique finally worked, and John grabbed the rod with both hands and braced himself against the transom. Nancy then took one of the engines out of gear to slow us down even more to help him fight the fish more easily. This striper had solidly hooked himself from the trolling speed of the boat. It then became imperative to maintain just enough forward headway to keep the fish hooked while John cranked the fish up to the boat.

My friend John is absolutely passionate about his fishing. As this was going to be his first Chesapeake Bay striper, I could tell he was quite excited.

"This fish is *really* pulling and feels great!"

"That's what I want to hear. Just hold on while Nancy gets us off the tunnel and away from all of these boats. Then we can try to land him."

During fall trolling for striped bass in the midst of a literal armada of small craft, the safest move once hooked up is to make a ninety-degree turn away from the bridge tunnel while "dragging" your fish with you. This gets you clear of the tunnel pilings, out of the pack of boats that can cut you off or tangle your rig, and into open water where you can fight and land your fish without unnecessary risks and worries. We would often reel in all the other lines to prevent any snags or tangles while our hooked fish would simply have to "hang" on the line until we could conclude the fight properly. Clearing the other rigs always paid handsome dividends in trolling time saved by avoiding down time from tangles or snags with the hooked fish or other boats.

Once we were in open water several hundred yards from the tunnel, my wife steered *Ocean Venture* toward the mouth of the bay while I finished reeling in the other trolling rigs. Next I moved to the stern to help John land his fish. He insisted on netting his fish so I handed him the net and took the rod. By now there was a beautiful twelve- to fourteen-pound striper on the surface zigzagging back and forth in a futile attempt to dislodge the hook from his mouth.

"John, here's what we'll do. I'm going to lead the fish up along the port side of the stern where you will already have the net immersed and then we'll take him, okay?"

"I'm ready to see this bass up close, but *don't lose my fish!*"

By virtue of his size, John enjoyed every advantage in reaching over the transom in order to net the fish as he stood 6'6" tall. One thing he did not count on, however, was the boat being rocked by a wave as he leaned over the stern with his feet planted on the damp cockpit deck.

WHEN THE WAVE HIT, John lost his balance and started to topple forward toward the water, almost as if in slow motion. Without thinking, I slammed the rod into a rod holder, braced myself, and used both hands to grab John's belt from behind while leaning backward and using all of my weight to keep him from falling into the bay.

"Hang on, John. I'm here to help you."

Somehow my 150 pounds sufficed to coax his 225 pounds back into the cockpit. John was still so excited I don't think he even realized how close he had come to swimming with his striper. As he regained his stance on the deck, he was staring at me and said, "Where's my fish, Mike?"

"I'm afraid I couldn't lead it to the net yet. We'll have to do it now."

Moments later, the two of us netted the fish. The fish landed on the deck and, after whipping around the cockpit for a few moments, gave me an opportunity to remove the well-secured jig from the corner of its mouth while John held the fish still. We threw the striper quickly into the Igloo cooler in the stern and slammed the lid shut. Then Nancy headed the boat back toward the tunnel to resume our striper trolling.

We continued to experience success with more stripers in the twelve- to fifteen-pound range and quickly approached our six fish limit for the day. After putting five bass in the cooler, we began releasing the rest of the fish, keeping one slot open just in case we lucked into a much larger striper. The fishing that day was so good that we thought we would have no problem picking up a large sixth fish. That monster striper never materialized, but we did catch one more striper of keeping size before calling it a day. We knew we would be looking forward to multiple delicious meals from the stripers we were fortunate enough to have caught. This was a fishing trip for striped bass I shall never forget, as it was the closest I have ever come to losing someone out of my boat in pursuit of a fish.

* * * *

THE DAYS WERE GROWING SHORTER, there was a distinct nip in the air, and it was approaching the height of striper season in late November. My neighbor Bill Cole and I had been out alone on *Ocean Venture* trolling hard all day with absolutely no success. We had worked our lures all the way from the first island of the Chesapeake Bay Bridge Tunnel almost to the eastern shore of Virginia on the opposite side of the bay. We had not seen any birds working and had only heard of one or two other fish being caught the entire day in spite of dozens of boats working the tunnel.

As I was going to be the fisherman in the boat that day, I quickly schooled Bill on how to run my twin-engine boat so we could troll safely and effectively. Bill is a 1957 U.S. Naval Academy graduate with twenty-eight years of naval experience, and he is highly knowledgeable in ship handling. This made him a quick study in small boat handling, and he was running *Ocean Venture* as well as I could within twenty minutes.

He had been masterful at his task of keeping us just up tide of the tunnel pilings so I could let our solitary lure sweep back into the zone where stripers were supposed to be waiting to ambush it. Unfortunately, as the day wore on, I felt like a total failure as I tried hard to achieve success for my friend on his first striped bass excursion in the bay. Bill was more than patient. I think he was just happy running the boat, enjoying the companionship, and being a "student fisherman." Regrettably, I did not feel like I had really taught him anything up to that point since we hadn't had a bite.

With about two hours of daylight remaining, I asked Bill to steer for the fourteen mile marker post on the bridge tunnel. When we arrived, we bundled up with sweaters, jackets, and wool caps as the sun was starting to drop toward the western horizon. As it was late in the day, most of the other boats had gone in, leaving just us and one other boat working the northern end of the tunnel.

"Well, Bill, let's give the fishing just one more try, if it's all right with you."

"Remember, I'm retired. There's nothing else I have planned for this evening."

By now the incoming tide had picked up to a pretty ferocious pace.

"Bill, do you feel confident steering the boat if we try to work in close to the tunnel right at that fourteen mile marker?"

"Piece of cake, Mike. Just tell me where to go and for how long."

"Once you get us parallel to the tunnel, I'm going to drop this wire line rig back until it hits bottom, and we'll see if anything happens."

With just two of us in the boat and only one of us fishing, I was only running the one rig, holding my wire line rod and reel in my hands at all times so we would have complete control and maneuverability regarding the bridge tunnel and any fish we might be fortunate enough to hook. If we snagged the tunnel, I knew Bill could immediately reverse course in a quasi-Williamson turn, enabling me to quickly free the lure. I was running my most tried and true rig, a white 1/8 ounce bucktail with a 7/0 hook trailing a piece of yellow Uncle Josh's pork rind. The rind had been carefully split down the middle to give it some good fluttering action. As cold as it was getting and as unproductive as the day had been, I was approaching the point of quitting. Something deep inside me, however, kept urging me to keep trying for a fish.

As soon as Bill brought the *Ocean Venture* parallel to the bridge tunnel fourteen mile marker, I asked him if he could still control the boat in the current on just one engine.

"Can do, Mike. No problem."

Within seconds of his response, the lead sinker ahead of our lure touched bottom and simultaneously the rod was almost pulled out of my hands as a strong fish peeled wire line off the reel and kept the clicker sounding. I leaned back hard to hold on.

"Bill, *fish on*, finally! Go ahead and turn away from the tunnel directly into the current. I'll just hang on until we have him clear of all the pilings." Bill made sure to avoid the one other boat that was working the same exact area we were and slowly motored us away from the tunnel. Once clear of the tunnel it was a long slow job to crank the weight of the fish in against his struggles and the strong force of the current. After about ten minutes I had a nice fat striper on the surface and called out to Bill.

"We're clear of everything, including that other boat. Just leave it in gear pointing straight into the current and step back here to help me land this fish."

When Bill stepped in the cockpit, I handed him the rod with the drag slacked off just enough to prevent losing the fish should it decide to make a break for it once he saw the boat. Bill carefully led the fish toward me so I could net it on the first try and lift it right onto the deck. I removed the bucktail jig from the striper's mouth and hoisted it into the cooler.

"William, what do you say we see if we can do that again, my friend?"

"Sounds good to me. Now I finally know what you've been talking about all day. That's a truly regal fish we just landed."

"Yeah, he probably goes about fifteen or sixteen pounds."

BILL RAN US RIGHT BACK to the same exact spot on the tunnel, and we repeated the drill at the same speed with the same lure and approach. Sure enough, we got the same result.

"Bill, *fish on again!* This one might even be heavier."

Without my even having to tell him this time, Bill turned *Ocean Venture* into the current and again worked us away from the tunnel while the fish slowly took line as I held on. I never want to horse one of these fish, particularly in strong current as it might be large enough to pull the hook and rip free with enough strain applied inadvertently. After I worked against the current to crank the fish all the way to the boat, my partner took his place in the cockpit and led our second striper head first into the now waiting net. When that fish landed on the deck, I looked at Bill, who seemed quite happy and said, "It's quite late, it's getting much colder by the minute, and we finally have a pair of nice eating-size stripers. Are you okay if we head for the dock?"

"That's fine, Mike. I've had a great day just being out here on the water in a small boat for a change. These two hard earned fish are just icing on the cake. Let's go home."

With few boats still out and a half hour of daylight remaining, Bill sped across the bay as I did some preliminary cleaning of the boat and dumped some ice on our two stripers.

Once we got home and cleaned the fish, we probably had a good twenty pounds of striper filets to share by the next day. The two of us had thoroughly enjoyed our bay bonding experience. I enjoyed listening to Bill's naval submarine stories, watching how quickly he took to small boat handling, and seeing him became an accomplished student of striped bass fishing in just one day.

* * * *

WE HAVE CAUGHT FISH AND MORE on occasion in some of the most unanticipated ways that an angler could ever imagine. One October day, John Reinhardt, Nancy, and I were out again on the Chesapeake Bay when we had such an event. Striper season had been open for just a few days, and it was a logistical nightmare to try to troll along the bridge tunnel. Even though we had a pretty early start on the fishing, there were more boats lined up along the pilings of the bridge tunnel than there would ever be at a boat show.

The considerate, polite, and sane fishermen were trolling in single file, hugging the pilings and then pulling away from the tunnel if they were lucky enough to hook up. In the midst of this attempt to maintain order, several boats were trolling under the overhead bridge roadway, running back and forth in slalom fashion between the pilings. In addition to this, on certain other boats, there were anglers we suspected were drinking more beer than seriously fishing. They were speeding up to cut in front of other boats or racing to descend on a spot where they just saw someone hook a fish. In many cases, these "rogue" boats were cutting across the boats' sterns. This inconsiderate action usually insured either snagging or cutting someone's trolling lines.

In the midst of this mayhem, my wife was handling the helm while John and I worked our two trolling rigs. I told John that if the fishing "free for all" continued, we would soon need to run just one rig with wire line only so we could have total control in the midst of the madness surrounding us. As the wire line sank more quickly, it would leave our trolling rig closer to *Ocean Venture* and be much less likely to be snagged. It would also be less likely to be cut off as the wire would cut through the monofilament of anyone inconsiderate enough to cut right behind our stern.

In this rodeo atmosphere, lots of four letter words began to fly from boat to boat as the small minority of inconsiderate fishermen began to cut anglers' rigs off. Not only did this madness cause anglers to lose time from fishing, but it was quite costly as some of the Stretch 25 lures being lost were not inexpensive items.

Just as I was telling John he would need to reel in his Penn 4/0 monofilament trolling rig, he exclaimed, "Mike, I think there's something on here, but it doesn't feel too lively."

"Just play it slowly while I pull in the wire line rig to get it out of the way."

As I cranked in about three hundred feet of wire line, I noticed that John was having a most difficult time dealing with whatever was on the end of his rod and reel. His 4/0 reel was loaded with plenty of forty-pound test monofilament, so I knew that he would not get spooled if he was patient as he attempted to regain line.

Finally I had all my wire retrieved, secured the rod and reel in a forward rod holder, and dropped the jig and leader in a bucket so we wouldn't trip over it.

"John, you need to get this fish in so we can get back to trolling."

"I'm really trying, but I'm having trouble regaining any line."

"Let me check that reel a moment."

When I gripped the rod John was using, all I felt was a lot of dead weight. I was not even sure he had hooked a fish. One time before, we had hooked something that felt similar and after a prolonged "fight," it turned out to be a ten pound diver's weight belt that had been lost under water.

"All right, here's what we're going to do. Put the rod in the stern holder, tighten the drag all the way and just start *winching* it in." John looked at me and said, "But I might lose my fish!"

"I don't think you will, but we have no other choice if we want to get back to our fishing."

After much hard cranking, most of the line was finally back on the reel. John was glad that almost all of the line was now retrieved since his arms were aching. I was standing in the stern, waiting for his catch to break the surface of the water. To the surprise of both of us, a medium weight rod and reel broke the surface! I leaned over the transom and pulled the rig into the boat. Except for saltwater exposure, it appeared to be no worse for wear, perhaps having been in the water only a few days as there was no real growth on it except for some green slime.

John said, "Look, isn't there some line still running out from the rod tip?"

"You're right, there is. Let's get it out of the bay so it doesn't foul someone's prop or get tangled around a sea turtle."

As I started to pull in the fishing line hand over hand, I felt weight on the other end. I figured maybe we'd get lucky and recover a nice trolling sinker.

After dumping a pile of monofilament on the cockpit deck, a nice healthy striped bass came into view, still well hooked on the original angler's hook.

"John, get the net. You really do have a striper here!"

The two of us quickly netted the fish and dumped him on the ice in the cooler.

"Whatever else happens out here today, I don't think you will be able to top that experience for a fish story."

John always told me that he enjoyed the challenge of the hunt or pursuit of the bass and the feel of the strike when the fish hit the lure. This had to be one distinctly different hit he would not soon forget. Even all of the good-sized striped bass we had caught couldn't top John's rod, reel, and bass catch of the day.

AND SO IN THE MIDST of striper mayhem on that day, we had benefited from another angler's loss. It was truly a fishing experience not likely to be repeated in our lifetime. Even my wife, Nancy, probably would not have believed that story if she had not witnessed it first hand.

Captain's Tip: If while trolling your lure becomes hung up on a piling of the Chesapeake Bay Bridge Tunnel, loosen the drag while you make a 180 degree turn and reverse your direction. As you reverse direction and reel in the loose line, more often than not, the lure will come free. Also, do not let out any more line than you need to just barely bounce bottom. The more line you have out, the greater the chance of getting snagged or hung up. Fish the *up tide* side of the tunnel and allow your lure to be swept back toward the pilings. If you do not hang up occasionally, your lure is probably not in the most productive strike zone.

For those who do not like competing with dozens of boats and freeing occasional hang ups, use binoculars to find a flock of diving birds in open water. Whenever approaching or leaving a school of fish where other boats are trolling, it is always good etiquette to go at slow speed and avoid cutting across the stern lines of other boats.

The author holding two striped bass.

13

Risky Dinner for Two

THE THREE TO FOUR FOOT WAVES built quickly, and the foaming white caps stood out starkly against the darkening sky. *Ocean Venture,* our thirty-two foot Wellcraft, suddenly began to pitch violently as the waves lifted the bow and slammed it into each following trough.

"I think it's time to pull in the lines and head in," my wife said.

We had paid more attention to fishing than we had to the suddenly approaching storm and were about to encounter a very rough ride back to Lynnhaven Inlet and the calmer waters of Long Creek.

The mackerel fishing had been *so* good that Nancy and I had not wanted to leave the waters off Cape Henry. Cape Henry is truly unique because anglers and boaters are constantly entertained by seasonal populations of dolphin, pelicans, cormorants, osprey, and occasionally sea turtles. A steady parade of Navy ships, commercial tankers, and private boats entering and exiting the bay must pass Cape Henry and its two sentinel lighthouses. The older brown brick lighthouse dates to the time of George Washington's presidency. Prior to its construction, the colonists resorted to lighting fires to mark the position of the Cape for ships. This lighthouse was actually built in 1791 with monies appropriated by Congress to provide a much needed and easily seen beacon for mariners to keep them from running aground as they entered and exited Chesapeake Bay. The original Cape Henry Lighthouse is no longer functional, but it is open to visitors who may climb it for a magnificent view of the bay area. On a clear day Chesapeake Light Tower, fourteen miles to the east, can actually be seen from the top of the original lighthouse. The newer, taller, distinctively black-and-white striped lighthouse is run by the U.S. Coast Guard and was constructed in 1881. It is this lighthouse that guides ships today with its beacon and impressively loud foghorn during haze or fog.

On the day that this particular fishing adventure was planned, Spanish mackerel would be our target species. Spanish mackerel normally make their annual appearance around Memorial Day and continue to be available through August. These speedy game fish sometimes linger into September if water temperatures remain around seventy to eighty degrees. The Virginia state record for this feisty species stands at eight pounds twelve ounces, while the world record is thirteen pounds. We hoped the fish we would catch would be in the two to four pound range. This size would make perfect fillets for the grill.

This was a trip where I would actually have a chance to fully relax, as Nancy consented to take the helm while we trolled around the ledges adjacent to the Cape. I would rig all the lures and watch the baits in the wake while sitting on a stern-facing boat seat. Little watching of the lures would be required since strikes in this type of fishing are normally quite loud and pronounced.

Whenever Nancy and I did this type of fishing we would head out quite early to beat the heat. With any luck, a lively tidal rip would form just off Cape Henry for at least a couple of hours on each tide. These rips are good news for anglers as they tumble hapless bait, attracting hungry predators such as Spanish mackerel. The fishing in the strong tidal area at the Cape can be outstanding not only in summer for Spanish mackerel, but also in January and February as huge striped bass school and exit the bay on their annual southern and offshore migrations. On occasion I have even caught tuna in these same ferocious tidal currents.

We began fishing as we passed the last of the Lynnhaven pound fishing nets just off the beach. I asked my wife to slow to trolling speed and steer parallel to the old T-shaped tower on the beach at Fort Story. This tower marks an area where the incoming or outgoing tide really starts to accelerate as huge volumes of water have to funnel in and out of the bay with the daily tides. From the tower all the way around the Cape to the two lighthouses and beyond to the harbormaster's building, I knew we would be in a hot strike zone for any prowling mackerel.

I always limit my trolling for mackerel to just two rigs. This minimizes the risk of any line tangles and allows me to quickly clear the lines for any strikes or turns. During full turns of the boat, I just grab one rod in each hand, cross both arms, and reverse their positions in the stern from port to starboard without any risk of a tangle. All this means more time for lures in the water and usually results in no down time and more fish in the box by the end of the trip.

The first rig I set up was a simple revolving spool Ambassador 5000 reel with twenty-pound test monofilament line. I set the drag on light strike, knowing how hard the mackerel usually hit and how the speed of the boat served to keep the fish hooked up. Once the first lure, a "00" silver Clark spoon, was in the water, I streamed it back about two-hundred feet behind the boat. If the frequency of the strikes decreased, I would drop the lure back as far as three-hundred feet and decrease the leader size to fifteen-pound test and use fluorocarbon leader. If strikes were still slow or infrequent, I would lengthen the leader to forty feet. Yes, this makes for a lot of reeling after a strike, but it also beats not catching fish!

After the first rig was set with the reel drag clicker on, I set about rigging the second rod.

For my "close to the boat" rig, I usually started with an eight-ounce torpedo sinker in front of the same lure and leader set up on the first rod. If it was a bright sunny day I put on a gold "00" Clark spoon. After a while, I switched both lures to the one getting the most strikes. The rig with the heavier sinker was let out only forty or fifty feet behind the boat, just beyond the edge of the propeller wash. Often, this lure would be hit much more frequently than the one farthest from the boat. Every day is different so it is always prudent to observe and then adjust.

On this day, no adjustments were needed. Within a minute of dropping the second rig in, *BANG, whirrrrrrrrr,* something took off with the first lure. After cranking it all the way to the boat, I swung an angry bluefish into the cooler and slammed the lid shut. This was a tell-tale sign for me to call out to Nancy.

"We're doing fine, but speed up about 200 or 300 RPM, and we should be able to get out of these small pesky blues."

"Okay, I've picked up speed to 1200 RPM," my wife shouted back over the noise of the engines.

"Now we should be able to eliminate the bluefish strikes and zero in on the mackerel because the blues won't be able to catch up with the lure at this speed."

Sure enough, within five minutes we had a fast, jarring run off on the rig closest to the boat. I could tell it was a mackerel as I cranked it in because it came right up to the surface and started to zigzag in a futile attempt to throw the lure. Mackerel always come up to the surface and show themselves while blues stay as deep as they can as long as they can. This fish, too, was swung into the fish cooler, where it beat rhythmically against the sides until it threw the Clark spoon from its mouth.

"Ummm, nice catch," Nancy said. "Now catch *your* dinner!"

I had long ago determined that it was much safer to wait the minute or so for these fish to give up the lure on their own than to risk removing the lure from a mouth full of razor sharp teeth while the fish struggled wildly in my hand.

As soon as I heard the lure break free and hit the side of the cooler, I carefully opened the cooler lid an inch and slid the lure out. Immediately I streamed the rig right back out behind the boat, returned the rod to the stern rod holder, and reset the drag on clicker for the next fish.

While Nancy steered the boat, this drill repeated itself dozens of times as we gradually filled the cooler with two- to three-pound Spanish mackerel. If the strikes slowed down, I would ask Nancy to start making very slow lazy S-turns with the boat. This effectively slowed down the speed of the lure on the side of the turn, often eliciting another strike. Another trick I would do myself or have Nancy do was to take the boat engines out of gear for four or five seconds and simply let *Ocean Venture* drift with the current. When we slowed, the Clark spoons would land on the bottom only to shoot up like a fleeing bait fish when we put the boat back in gear. This, too, produced several of the day's better sized mackerel.

BY EARLY AFTERNOON we had all the fish we could use for dinner and a whole batch more for the freezer. Unfortunately the wind had been steadily increasing, and I was forced to spend the last hour of fishing kneeling in the cockpit as I continued to crank in fat and feisty Spanish mackerel. As each fish hit and tore off line, I held on to the gunwale with my left hand while cranking in the line with my right. I was reluctant to stand up in the cockpit because the building waves were hitting the boat and causing it to rock severely even though my wife was maintaining headway while steering at the helm. Nancy had been scanning the darkening horizon to the west and had no interest in dealing with the clearly approaching weather front and thunderstorm. After a quick discussion, I rapidly reeled in the two trolling rigs and took over at the helm. With plenty of fresh mackerel in the cooler, the two of us made the overdue decision to call it a day and head for port.

I complimented my wife on her rough weather boat handling skills that had allowed me to catch so many mackerel and steered the boat in the direction of the dark wall of clouds to the west. As I turned the wheel hard to port, the starboard side of the boat was slammed by a sustained burst of wind that caused us to heel over dangerously. I gripped the wheel tightly and continued to apply throttle until full control of the boat was mine again. We had just completed a ninety degree full speed turn as we headed into the approach lane to Lynnhaven Inlet. As we raced toward the day marker at the entrance, we both knew we had overstayed our time at the Cape. The urgency to return to port was evidenced by cold rain drops beating on the windshield and the canvas top in contrast to the wilting heat that we had experienced. The wind that had struck us so hard was clearly the downburst from the front edge of the thunderstorm. We were barely able to reach the safety of the inlet in front of the rapidly approaching squall line. Thankfully, after a short trip down Long Creek, we tied up at our dock at Marina Shores just as the brunt of the storm hit, but we were still excited about our day's success on the water even though we were drenched.

As we drove home, I thought back to other fishing experiences I had been fortunate enough to have had in Hawaii, the Caribbean, and Alaska. With so many great fishing days like this day in our bay waters, I told myself that my all time favorite place to fish was, and always would be, right here in Virginia Beach.

Captain's Tip: Even if the sky is clear at the beginning of your fishing trip, keep a sharp eye on the weather, especially when distracted by excellent fishing. There are some old fishermen and a lot of bold fishermen, but there are very few old, bold fishermen.

Captain's Note: Both lighthouses at Cape Henry are a few hundred feet from each other on the U.S. Army base at Fort Story. The base and the lighthouses are accessible to the public after visitors first undergo a security check at the Eighty-ninth Street gate in Virginia Beach. Surf fishing is permitted in designated areas by obtaining a base fishing permit in addition to a Virginia saltwater fishing license.

Appendix A
Spanish Mackerel Captain's Tips

- Place a small plastic bead in line before tying on terminal rigs. It will protect your rod tip.
- Only use coastlock swivels. They are unlikely to open under pressure.
- Use barrel or ball bearing swivels in trolling leaders to prevent line twist, which causes a lure to spin creating an unnatural presentation.
- Troll with the lightest leader possible. I like 30-pound test for Spanish mackerel. Use 15-pound test if strikes are infrequent.
- Fluorocarbon line is worth using where the lure is attached to the leader. Spanish mackerel have *excellent* vision!
- Twenty feet is a good starting length for a Spanish mackerel leader. Place a swivel at the front end of the leader and also tie one into the middle of the leader. Be sure to use black swivels or you may lose some lures to fish that think a silver swivel is a small baitfish. Tie lures directly to the monofilament line *without* any type of metal clip.
- Use a clinch or improved clinch knot to tie the lure to the line.
- Pre-make trolling rigs and store them on round plastic leader spools. This makes for neat, easy storage and allows quick set-up.
- A good all-around lure to start with is the "00" Clark spoon in silver. If it is very sunny, try the same spoon in gold. If the bait fish in the area look larger, try the next two larger sizes of Clark spoons to match the bait.
- Don't be afraid to lengthen the leader. I have used as much as forty feet of leader if fish are reluctant to hit. A good rule of thumb is "The slower the fishing, the longer the leader!"
- If hits are slow, drop your last lure way, *way* back (try several hundred feet). It will usually make a difference.
- Always maintain forward speed with the boat when hooked up. The constant pull on the fish makes it much more difficult for it to throw the lure. Do slow down after a strike, but always maintain some minimum forward motion.

- If hook ups are scarce, try using a small "bird" about five feet in front of your lure. Color is not as critical as commotion in the water.
- Experiment by using a different size lure and trolling sinker on each rod until you find the best producer for the day. Then switch to the one that works best.
- Try trolling with the current and against it. Take special note of what your speed is as well as the direction of the current when hits occur.
- If there is a rip, troll along the edges of it. The clear side is usually better. Pay attention to water temperature changes. This is "structure" for fish, just like a ledge.
- Keep a log. Record date, stage of tide, trolling direction, bait in the water, water temperature, water clarity, lures used, catch results, etc. You can learn a great deal from analyzing this data, and it will prove invaluable in successive seasons.

Appendix B
Boat and Angler Friendly
Leaders for Shark Fishing

WHEN FISHING FOR SHARKS, a safe, easy-to-handle leader that will hold up and not harm your boat hull is essential. Many shark fishermen use either plain wire or cable leader. There is a better, safer leader. Try using 1/8" plastic or nylon covered cable (outer diameter 3/16") and 500-pound class swivels. Cut copper air conditioning tubing (3/8" O.D., ¼" I.D.) in one-inch lengths with a hack saw to make crimping sleeves for the cable. The sleeves can easily be squeezed in a vise until they are the correct oval shape to accept two sections of the cable. This will form a loop for crimping at each end to secure swivels and finish the leader ends. Detergent or liquid soap will help the sleeves slide over the cable prior to crimping. Crimp a 500-pound barrel swivel to the "rod end" of the leader. Crimp a 500-pound coastlock style swivel to the "hook rig end" of the leader. Purists may choose to use small stainless shackles (available in boating stores) in conjunction with barrel swivels instead of coastlock swivels which could conceivably open. Twelve feet of leader (plus your hook rig's length) will serve to keep shark tails from breaking your line. If you are worried about sharks rolling up in the leader, go up to fifteen or more feet. Be sure, however, to check the latest IGFA leader regulations should you be seeking record fish.

Crimping is easily accomplished with a swaging tool or a hammer and punch to make alternating crimps on the copper sleeves. Be sure to crimp over both parts of the cable that form the leader loop. To be really safe, I would also alternate the indents or crimps on opposite sides of each sleeve for maximum strength. The resulting leaders are virtually indestructible, easy to make, and absolutely will not kink. They are also much safer and easier to grip than plain wire or cable leaders and much less likely to harm your boat's hull during the end game. For safety reasons, do continue to wear gloves when leadering a shark, even though these leaders are easier to grip. I have never had a crimp on one of these leaders pull out. The leaders have lasted nicely and definitely proven themselves through years of hard use, including many sharks in the four-, five-, and six-hundred pound range up to and including a 673 pound Virginia state record dusky shark.

Happy shark fishing!

Appendix C
Trolling Tips to Increase Your Catch

- Fish early or late in day: bite is usually best then.
- Troll no more than two rigs in congested areas or if you are going to be changing directions. Tangles you will avoid will make it more than worthwhile in fishing time gained!
- Use release clips to get the angle of line as low to the water as possible. Black's are good; Aftco Roller Trollers are best. Outriggers work well for a surface or slightly subsurface lure.
- Best all around spoon to pull is Clark's Silver #00 RBMS.
- Use fluorocarbon line on trolling leaders (low visibility).
- Make up a variety of leader sizes: 60-pound = good to start, easy to handle at boat. Work down to 30, 20, 15 if not getting hits. (The clearer the water is, the lighter the leader.)
- Try fishing the warmer side of a rip or tide-line if there is a temperature difference.
- Use long leaders = start with twenty-five to thirty feet. Game fish have excellent eyesight. Go longer if not getting hits.
- Always use a barrel or ball bearing swivel in the middle of each leader to counteract line twist.
- One leader end should have a Coastlock snap swivel. The other end has the lure. This combats line twist, too, and improves lure action.
- All hardware (snaps, swivels) should be black to prevent hits and bite offs away from the lure.
- Try trolling with the current, against the current, and cross current to see which is more productive.
- Start trolling with: one leader on eight ounce in-line trolling sinker—keep close to boat (maybe let out fifty to seventy-five feet). Attach one leader to a two or three ounce sinker about one hundred yards back.
- The farther back you set your far rig from the boat, the more hits you will get. You cannot troll a lure too far behind the boat.
- Pull leaders in hand over hand. Once you get the fish near the

boat, keep it coming and pull it up in one continuous lifting motion, never releasing the line tension.

- Drop fish and lure right into the cooler and close the lid. (Frequently the fish will release itself from the lure after rattling around in the cooler.)
- If hits are slow, try zig-zagging, slow "S" turns, and going to neutral for four or five seconds to allow lures to drop to bottom. Often they will be hit as you come up off the bottom as you start up or on the way down when you slow down. Don't be afraid to experiment: increasing or decreasing trolling speed may be the magic ticket.
- On very bright sunny days try the Gold #00 Clark's Spoon. Your strikes may increase over silver lures.
- Try a small offshore bird about five feet in front of a spoon. This can make a big difference on a slow day or make a good day even better.

Appendix D
Baits for Flounder Fishing

SQUID BAIT
- Start the day with squid cut into thin pennant-like strips with a split tail.
- Use large, whole, cleaned squid and use the whitest squid available.
- Always hook the squid strip as close to the end of the strip as possible.
- Avoid creating a second "flap" of bait folding backward since this will make the bait appear *unnatural* as it works through the water.

FISH BAIT
- Use live minnows or spot as your first choice.
- Use fresh flounder, but save the carcass to prove your bait came from a *legal*-size flounder.
- Berkley Gulp artificial minnows work great on a small hook or a jig. Dip the bait in the scent solution each time it is used.
- The white underbelly from bluefish, Spanish mackerel, or shark is excellent bait when cut in strips. Shark underbelly is the most durable.
- Try dipping any of the above baits in Gulp scent solution or spraying new or used bait with menhaden oil to increase its attraction.
- Cut baits from the belly areas of spot, croaker or rays also work well.
- Replace cut bait every twenty minutes with a new fresh bait.

HOW TO RIG BAIT
- Hook minnows through both lips or through the eye sockets.
- Hook live spot through both lips or in the dorsal area.
- Put a squid strip or fish strip bait on the hook *after* hooking a minnow to *lock* the live bait on the hook. Minnows will stay on the hook and last longer this way.

- A fish hooked toward its tail will tend to swim toward the bottom where the flounder are located.

CAPTAIN'S TRICK

Add a strip of Uncle Josh's # 50 yellow or white pork rind on the hook to prevent a flounder from biting off the back of strip baits and missing the hook. The pork rind also provides something for the fish to *hang on to* until it eats its way up to the hook.

CAPTAIN'S TRICK

Use a double hook sliding rig to catch short strikers and lay the bait *flat* once hooked so it will flutter in the water.

CAPTAIN'S TRICK

Fillet all strip baits to 1/8" thickness and slit the tail of the bait halfway up for maximum flutter and attraction.

Appendix E
Information about Sport Fishing
in Virginia Beach

The following groups can provide information about deep-sea sport fishing, boat charters, pier and surf fishing, and boat ramps.

Virginia Beach Visitor Information Center
1-800-822-3224
or
757-437-4882
or
www.vbfun.com

Virginia Saltwater Fishing Tournament
757-491-5160
or
mrcswt@visi.net

Virginia Beach Conventions and Visitors Bureau
757-385-4700
or
www.vbfun.com

Virginia Aquarium and Marine Science Center
(Information on seasonal whale and dolphin watching trips)
757-385-7777
or
www.virginiaaquarium.com

VIRGINIA MARINE

SPECIES	WEIGHT
Albacore	68 lbs.
Amberjack	118 lbs.
Barracuda	45 lbs. 8 oz.
Bluefish	25 lbs. 4 oz.
Cobia	104 lbs. 8 oz.
Cod, Atlantic	35 lbs.
Crevalle Jack	48 lbs. 12 oz.
Croaker	5 lbs. 13 oz.
Dolphin	71 lbs. 8 oz.
Drum, Black	111 lbs.
Drum, Red	85 lbs. 4 oz.
False Albacore	25 lbs. 4 oz.
Flounder	17 lbs. 8 oz.
Kingfish (Roundhead)	2 lbs. 13 oz.
Mackerel, King	52 lbs. 2 oz.
Mackerel, Spanish	9 lbs. 13 oz.
Marlin, Blue	1,093 lbs. 12 oz.
Marlin, White	131 lbs. 10 oz.
Pollock	23 lbs. 8 oz.
Pompano	5 lbs. 10 oz.
Porgy	5 lbs. 5 oz.
Sailfish	68 lbs. 8 oz.
Sea Bass	10 lbs. 4 oz.
Shark, Bigeye Thresher	149 lbs.
Shark, Blacktip	76 lbs. 10 oz.
Shark, Blue	266 lbs.
Shark, Bull	256 lbs.
Shark, Dusky	673 lbs.
Shark, Hammerhead (Great)	430 lbs.
Shark, Hammerhead (Scalloped)	245 lbs.
Shark, Hammerhead (Smooth)	272 lbs.
Shark, Lemon	312 lbs. 12 oz.
Shark, Mako	728 lbs.
Shark, Sandbar (Brown)	213 lbs.
Shark, Sand Tiger	339 lbs.
Shark, Silky	110 lbs.
Shark, Spinner	129 lbs. 8 oz.
Shark, Thresher	525 lbs.
Shark, Tiger	1,099 lbs. 12 oz.
Shark, White	131 lbs.
Sheepshead	20 lbs. 12 oz.
Spadefish	13 lbs.
Spot	2 lbs. 6 oz.
Striped Bass	63 lbs 8 oz.
Swordfish	381 lbs. 8 oz.
Tarpon	130 lbs.
Tautog	24 lbs.
Trout, Gray	19 lbs.
Trout, Speckled	16 lbs.
Tuna, Bigeye	285 lbs. 12 oz.
Tuna, Blackfin	33 lbs. 15 oz.
Tuna, Bluefin	398 lbs. 8 oz.
Tuna, Skipjack	22 lbs. 11 oz.
Tuna, Yellowfin	203 lbs. 12 oz.
Wahoo	109 lbs.

GAME FISH RECORDS

WHERE	WHEN	ANGLER
Norfolk Canyon	1992	Irvin Fenton, Jr.
Ches. Light Tower	1986	Mark J. Roberts
CB Buoy Line	1996	Wayne Seymour
Bluefish Rock	1986	Gayle E. Cozzens
Ches. Bay Br. Tunnel	2002	Steve Hasynic
Off Wachapreague	1969	Robert Crammer
Ches. Light Tower	1993	Charles McCaskill, III
The Cell (Ches. Bay)	1982	Jim Mitchem
Off Virginia Beach	1991	Don Dorey
Off Cape Charles	1973	Betty D. Hall
Wreck Island	1981	Herman Moore
Off Virginia Capes	1964	Jack Sparrow
Baltimore Channel	1971	Charles E. Cross
Off Sandbridge	2002	Chip Watters
Off Virginia Beach	1999	Andrew John Allessio
Off Virginia Beach	1993	Everett Cameron
Norfolk Canyon	1978	Edward Alan Givens
Off Virginia Beach	1978	Rudolph D.van't Riet
Off Chincoteague	1998	Lee Michalski
Scarborough Island	1992	Robert T. Long
Off Chincoteague	1978	Charles B. Haines, Sr.
Off Virginia Beach	1977	P. J. Murden
Off Virginia Beach	2000	Allan P. Paschall
The Cigar	1992	Wayne M. Gross
Off Virginia Beach	1988	John W. Thurston, Jr.
The Cigar	1987	Wayne C. DeFord
V-Buoy	1982	Craig R. Paige
S.E. Lumps	1982	Michael J. Halperin
S.E. Lumps	1984	Ronald E. Ault
The Cigar	1977	Don Lips
Off Virginia Beach	1988	Carolyn L. Matthews
Off Sandbridge	1976	Bill Walker
Ches. Light Tower	1983	Geoffrey H. Newbill
Triangle Wrecks	1986	Bill Moffett
Off Cape Charles	1983	Kelly D. Capps
Nofolk Canyon	1977	Gary W. Seay
Off Chincoteague	1991	John E. Patton, II
Triangle Wrecks	2004	Andrew P. Schuyler
S.E. Lumps	1981	John W. Thurston, Jr.
S.E. Lumps	1981	Fred Williams
CBBT, Seagull Fishing Pier	2005	Arun Nhek
The Cell (Ches. Bay)	1988	Otis Tribble
Off Poquoson	1980	Nathan Dryden
Off Wachapreague	2005	Paul Klekner
Norfolk Canyon	1978	James D. Alexander
Off Oyster	1975	Barry Truitt
Off Wachapreague	1987	Gregory R. Bell
Ches. Bay Br. Tunnel	1983	Philip W. Halstead
Masons Beach	1977	Bill Katko
Norfolk Canyon	2003	Melvin Bray
Norfolk Canyon	2004	William W. Charlton, III
The Fingers	2003	E. K. Morrison
The Cigar	1995	Kitty Falk
Norfolk Canyon	1981	Bruce C. Gottwald, Jr.
Off Virginia Beach	1994	Delmo Dawson

Acknowledgments

MANY PEOPLE PLAYED A PART in my "angling growth" which indirectly led to this book becoming a reality. Sincere thanks and gratitude are in order for my in house editor, my wife, Nancy. I now totally know the meaning of the term rewrite!

Some talented fishermen who helped determine the outcome of some of these adventures were John Thurston, Craig Paige, Jimmy Stokes, David Tugwell, Keith Casiano, Jim Hunter, and Randy Parker. Thanks to each of you for serving as mentors.

Claude Bain, in his capacity as the former director of the Virginia Saltwater Fishing Tournament, was most helpful in verifying historical records and providing general fishing information as needed. Claude's help is most appreciated. Special thanks to Lewis Gillingham, current tournament director, for sharing his insights on striped bass.

I must thank Lynnhaven Marine-Boatel and Fisherman's Wharf Marina for all their able assistance as weigh stations and official certification of many trophy fish.

Thanks are also in order for John Gallegos, wildlife biologist at Back Bay National Wildlife Refuge. His unique tide and ecology items have greatly enriched this work.

To the many friends, anglers, and acquaintances who have fished with me over the years, I also express my thanks. Without your presence and assistance, many of the described adventures would never have taken place.

Many thanks to the following people at Dorrance Publishing Company for their excellent guidance in bringing *True Tales of the Tide* to print: Ray Nikolaison, Patricia Turley, Sarah Quigley, and Sarah Vine.

Finally I again need to thank my parents for convincing me from an early age that if something is worth doing, it is worth doing right.